Jim Haynes is a first-generation Aussie whose mother migrated from the UK as a child during the Depression. His father arrived on a British warship at the end of World War II, met his mother and stayed. 'My parents always insisted we were Australian, not British,' says Jim.

Educated at Sydney Boys High and Sydney Teachers' College, he taught for six years at Menindee, on the Darling River, and later at high schools in northern New South Wales and in London. He has also worked in radio and as a nurse, cleaner and sapphire salesman, and has two degrees in literature from the University of New England and a master's degree from the University of Wales in the UK.

Jim formed the Bandy Bill & Co Bush Band in Inverell in 1978. He also worked in commercial radio and on the popular ABC *Australia All Over* program. In 1988 he signed as a solo recording artist with Festival Records, began touring and had a minor hit with 'Mow Ya Lawn'. Other record deals followed, along with hits like 'Since Cheryl Went Feral' and 'Don't Call Wagga Wagga Wagga'.

Having written and compiled 26 books, released many albums of songs, verse and humour and broadcast his weekly Australiana segment on Macquarie Radio for fifteen years, Jim was awarded the Order of Australia Medal in 2016 'for service to the performing arts as an entertainer, author, broadcaster and historian'. He lives at Moore Park in Sydney with his wife, Robyn.

# BEST AUSTRALIAN
# DRINKING
# STORIES

## ALSO BY JIM HAYNES

*The Big Book of Verse for Aussie Kids*
*Best Australian Racing Stories*
*The Great Australian Book of Limericks* (2nd ed.)
*The Best Australian Trucking Stories*
*The Best Australian Sea Stories*
*The Best Australian Bush Stories*
*The Best Australian Yarns*
*Australia's Best Unknown Stories*
*The Best Gallipoli Yarns and Forgotten Stories*
*The Big Book of Australian Racing Stories*
*Australia's Most Unbelievable True Stories*
*Great Australian Scams, Cons and Rorts*

# BEST AUSTRALIAN
# DRINKING
# STORIES

## JIM HAYNES

ALLEN&UNWIN
SYDNEY·MELBOURNE·AUCKLAND·LONDON

Allen & Unwin
83 Alexander Street
Crows Nest NSW 2065
Australia
Phone: (61 2) 8425 0100
Email: info@allenandunwin.com
Web: www.allenandunwin.com

A catalogue record for this
book is available from the
National Library of Australia

ISBN 978 1 76063 290 8

Set in 12/15 pt Minion Pro by Midland Typesetters, Australia
Printed and bound in Australia by Griffin Press

10 9 8 7 6 5 4 3 2 1

The paper in this book is FSC® certified.
FSC® promotes environmentally responsible,
socially beneficial and economically viable
management of the world's forests.

*This book is for Amber, Corky, Robyn, Grant, BigRuss, Les, Nick et al. They know why.*

# CONTENTS

# INTRODUCTION

'In Australia there is always the refuge of a regular booze-up with the boys. Suspicion of one's peers is thus temporarily dissolved in plenty of alcohol—Australia's national solvent.'

Ronald Conway, author and psychologist, 1976

This book is an attempt to tell the history of Australia's almost-250-year love affair with alcohol, using stories, verse and some fascinating historical narratives.

As far as the historical pieces are concerned, I can vouch for their accuracy—I researched and wrote them all!

Alcohol has played a major, quite disproportionate, role in the history of our nation since 1769 and I find that fascinating. I also find it quite informative when we come to analyse and understand our 'national character', legislation and law making, and our social history and accepted cultural attitudes over those 250 years.

Researching and retelling the alcohol-related history of Cook's voyages, the First Fleet, the Rum Rebellion, the mutiny of the 99th Regiment, the soldiers' riot of 1916 and the effects of six o'clock closing has been an enlightening exercise for me. I now understand, just a little better, the society in which I grew up.

Exploring the impact on our alcoholic history of characters like James Cook, Joseph Banks, John Macarthur, James Squire, William Bligh, Lachlan Macquarie, Peter Degraves and others has made me develop a true admiration for some of them, a grudging admiration for others and an understanding of just how wicked and self-serving some of our founding fathers were.

Researching the history of pubs in Australia has truly been an exercise in understanding the social history of our nation. When I was a young man, there was a pub on every corner in the CBD of Sydney. Different professions frequented different pubs and each had its own flavour.

In my college days, an end-of-term pub crawl started at the White Horse in King Street, Newtown, and progressed down Broadway and then along George Street to finish at the Ship Inn. To finish took a mighty effort, even when we restricted ourselves to one side of the road. Faint hearts didn't last past Central Railway Station.

Today I imagine it would be difficult to become inebriated doing a pub crawl along that same route. The majority of those pubs, including the White Horse, no longer exist. Sydney has truly undergone a reformation of drinking establishments, as have most cities.

A parallel reformation has occurred in country towns. In many small towns, pub licences have been transferred and towns have lost their only local pub. For all their faults, these pubs were often the communal heart of the town and these smaller towns are now rather sad, often dying, communities.

In larger country towns, pubs have lost their original character and their differences. These pubs once catered to different clientele, such as the Commercial for travelling salesmen and businessmen, and the Railway, close to the station, for train travellers and railway men. Graziers and loyalists frequented the Royal, the Empire or the Imperial, while the Australian was often the chosen haunt of shearers and 'Labor men'. Pubs were also defined by the football codes and sports they supported, and each had its own character for all these reasons. But when six o'clock closing was introduced in 1916, it altered the nature of pubs and took away many of the unique characteristics of individual establishments, and today the differences are mostly gone, replaced by generic bars, bistros and gaming rooms.

As for the stories and verses by some of my favourite authors that make up the bulk of this collection, well, I think they often tell the alcoholic history of Australia as well as, if not better than, the history lessons do.

Many of the stories concern people getting 'roaring drunk'. This expression is used to indicate that those who are inebriated are having a rollicking good time, becoming outrageous, reckless and daring as opposed to introverted, depressive and vindictive.

Rightly or wrongly, this is the type of drunkenness that has been tolerated, forgiven and even rather admired by a large section of Australian society for about two hundred years. It is a type of drunkenness associated with good times, mateship, camaraderie, nostalgia and outrageous, though often amusing, social behaviour.

Of course, it is also the same type of drunkenness that a sober person finds extremely childish and often boorish. Arriving late at a boozy party is never a good idea if you want to feel close to, and comfortable with, your fellow human beings.

In Australia there has too often been a forgiveness of drunken behaviour and a feeling of warmth and concern for the drinker. Drunken deeds often become the stuff of local or family legend. There is a real affection for the uncle or mate who is amusing or outrageous when he's 'had a few'. The cultural shame associated with social drunkenness that one finds in Asia and many European countries was almost nonexistent in the Australia of my youth.

Why is this? Well, there are many probable reasons for the toleration of this form of drunkenness in Australia.

You could argue that Australia had fewer social restrictions and patterns built up over generations than other nations, or that Australia was, by its nature as a migrant and convict settlement, bound to develop social traits that opposed authority and conformity.

However it developed, Australian society still has a very tolerant attitude towards alcohol and a strong suspicion of intolerant or 'wowserish' attitudes to drinking.

The more bohemian of the *Bulletin* writers considered the temperance movement to be a bunch of interfering nuisances who should stop telling others how to live. Bartlett Adamson described a wowser this way in a little ditty entitled 'Wow, Sir!':

The wowser is a mean pervert,
He has an evil eye.
He keeps his brain-pan full of dirt,
And murmurs, 'Let us pry.'

Henry Lawson's drinking mate, Victor Daley, penned this amusing little poem called 'Lullaby':

Oh, hush thee, my baby, the time it has come,
For the nuisance to pass here with trumpet and drum.
Oh fear not the bugle, though loudly it blows—
'Tis the Salvation Army disturbs thy repose.

Artist and author Norman Lindsay, who drew the definitive caricatures of wowsers, declared that Christianity itself was a 'communist uprising of the underworld that sought to destroy . . . all that the word civilization can mean.'

The need to be a drinker to be fully included in the male-dominated society of working-class Australia was, until recently, a very palpable social force. The Barry Humphries quote, 'Never trust a man who doesn't drink', which prefaces one of the stories in this collection, is still a commonly held belief, whether originally intended satirically or not.

Some of the stories in this collection celebrate the social gift of alcohol. Riotous evenings of complete surrender to Bacchus, or business deals sealed with booze, grave social occasions subverted by drink—and Henry Lawson's apology and justification for alcoholism.

Pieces by Lennie Lower and Kenneth Cook, which meet the criteria described above, appear a combined total of nine times in this collection and it is interesting to note that Lower was, like Lawson, a quite serious alcoholic, while Ken Cook called himself a 'lay alcoholic'.

For Lower, the subject of drink provided yet another chance for social satire, wordplay and cynicism. While I have found his attitude to be typical of many intelligent hard drinkers, few of them wrote as well, or as amusingly, as Lennie.

Kenneth Cook was a particularly accurate observer of outback life and while his stories here are humorous accounts of alcohol-related incidents, you can detect also a sense of the acceptance of alcohol as a part of a 'normal' life.

Some stories are salutary tales which deal with the consequences of getting 'roaring drunk': the hangovers, sufferings and recriminations of the regular binge drinker, the physical and psychological results of drinking—the harsh realities.

I was taught to have respect and sympathy for drunks as a kid mainly because of a quirk of history. When I was a kid many drunks and 'derelicts', as they were often called back then, were also 'returned men', veterans of World War II or even World War I.

I am sure that a general awareness of the horrors of war and their effects on some 'returned men' played a part in further developing a tolerance of drunks throughout the 1920s and 1930s, and, after World War II, the 1950s. I developed some small understanding of the dreadful realities of a drunkard's day-to-day life by observing various local drunks as a kid and later, as a school teacher in small country towns, talking to some of them and getting to know them.

Some of these stories represent the darker side of drinking and alcoholism; some are accounts of people finally facing some harsh alcoholic reality—either private or social.

The Roman proverb, *in vino veritas*, came to mind as I prepared this collection. The idea of truth being revealed via alcohol has been used in stories included here by authors like Gavin Casey, Jacqueline Kent, 'The Sandman' and Frank Daniel.

The various Australian social rituals associated with alcohol range from ethnic to gastronomic and from religious to barbaric. We are always being asked to raise our glasses to something. The old pagan use of alcohol as a method of pledging and bonding is alive and well Down Under.

So, here is a collection of history, anecdotes, stories, verse and literature about Australian drinking. I hope it is a collection that is amusing, informative, entertaining and thought-provoking. I hope it is a collection that will neither drive you to drink nor turn you away from the pleasures of alcohol in moderation.

So, please, grab a glass of your favourite beverage and read on.

*Jim Haynes*
*2018*

# A TOAST TO TEMPERANCE

**Anonymous**

> Here's to a Temperance Dinner,
> With water in glasses tall
> And cups of tea to end with
> And me . . . not there at all!

# SECTION ONE
# A NATIONAL PASTIME

# THE ALCOHOLICS' CREED

**Anonymous**

Our lager
Which art in barrels
Hallowed be thy foam
Thy will be drunk
Thy pints be sunk
At home as it is in tavern.
Give us this day thy foamy head
And forgive us our spillages
As we forgive those who spill thee against us
And lead us not to incarceration
But deliver us from hangovers
For thine is the sin done, the headache, the guilt trip,
For ever and ever . . .
. . . barmen

# THE ALCOHOLIC HISTORY OF AUSTRALIA

## Jim Haynes

> 'Instead of looking back on our past as a
> continual riot, we should see it rather as
> a series of alcoholic spasms.'
>
> Sidney J. Baker, 1945

The European history of Australia is incredibly alcoholic.

The Australian character seems to be inextricably linked to alcohol. 'Easy-going', 'tolerant' and 'fond of a drink' are qualities, indeed clichés, that occur again and again when Australian stereotypes are being portrayed both at home and overseas. Let's not forget that we had a quite popular prime minister who included among his achievements being the world champion beer drinker during his time as a Rhodes Scholar at Oxford University. Bob Hawke was immortalised in the 1954 Guinness Book of Records for drinking a yard of ale (2.5 pints or 1.4 litres) in eleven seconds.

Did this national reputation develop as a result of the pioneer, rough-and-ready nature of our first hundred years of European settlement? Was it allied to the large percentage of Irish and cockney migrants, who already had a long-established 'drinking culture', in those early years of the colonies? Or was it more to do with the male-dominated nature of Australian frontier society in the 19th century?

Of course, it is possible to argue quite simplistically that, with a population consisting entirely of convicts, soldiers, sailors and children born out of wedlock in prison hulks or in transit, the First Fleet set a national trend for drunkenness and tolerance of alcohol that could never be entirely reversed.

It should be understood, however, that the British settled on this continent at a time when there was an extraordinarily widespread acceptance of alcohol throughout British society. This was especially evident in the navy. You have only to read accounts of British naval and merchant voyages in the 18th and 19th centuries to understand the huge role played by 'grog'—chiefly rum, or brandy for officers—in the daily life of a British vessel.

Reading accounts of Captain Cook's voyages gives a special insight. Considered a very firm and fair commander, Cook encouraged the making and consumption of fruit-based home brew (a 'jungle juice' that may or may not have helped ward off scurvy) and his crew were very often more drunk than sober. The German botanist Johann Forster, who went on Cook's second voyage, described the crew as 'solicitous to get very drunk, though they are commonly solicitous about nothing else'.

They certainly knew how to celebrate on Cook's first voyage. If we look at the journal of Sir Joseph Banks, who was known as 'the father of Australia' in the early days of our European history, we can see the beginnings of the Aussie tradition of celebrating Christmas with alcohol.

The *Endeavour* was off the north coast of New Zealand's North Island, near Three Kings Island, in late December 1769. Here are Banks's entries, verbatim:

1769 December 24. Land in sight, an Island or rather several small ones . . . Calm most of the Day: myself in a boat shooting in which I had good success, killing chiefly several Gannets or Solan Geese so like European ones that they are hardly distinguishable from them. As it was the humour of the ship to keep Christmas in the old fashiond way it was resolvd of them to make a Goose pye for tomorrow's dinner.

> 1769 December 25. Christmas day: Our Goose pie was eat with great approbation and in the Evening all hands were as Drunk as our forefathers used to be upon the like occasion.
>
> 1769 December 26. This morn all heads ached with yesterdays debauch. Wind has been Easterly these 3 or 4 days so we have not got at all nearer the Island than we were.

So the tone for celebrating a southern hemisphere Christmas in mid-summer in good alcoholic fashion was set—even before Cook claimed the east coast of Australia for Britain!

Of course, alcohol and drunkenness have been around almost as long as so-called 'civilisation'. Appreciation of alcohol is one blessing, among many, passed down to other Western civilisations by the ancient Greeks. The American writer and observer of human behaviour Ambrose Bierce (1842–1914) described Bacchus as 'a convenient deity invented by the ancients as an excuse for getting drunk'. But he also noted that alcohol was not a feature of all cultures: 'When pitted against the hard-drinking Christians the abstemious Mahometans go down like grass before the scythe.'

And his comment on British colonisation was: 'In India one hundred thousand beef-eating and brandy-and-soda-guzzling Britons hold in subjection two hundred and fifty million vegetarian abstainers of the same Aryan race.'

Bierce's literary trademark was, of course, cynicism.

Nevertheless, it was this British society, largely accepting of alcoholic excess, that established colonies in Australia between 1788 and 1836, and it was the British Navy and merchant fleet, with their easy acceptance of drunkenness as part of everyday life, that provided the only real link between Europe and those colonies.

Our national day is 26 January, the day the ships of the First Fleet moved from Botany Bay to Port Jackson, the male convicts were disembarked and the British flag was raised. We should, perhaps, spare a thought for 6 February as a more appropriate national day. On the evening of that day, following the disembarkation of the female convicts and extra rations of rum all round, there developed, in the words of historian Manning Clark, 'a drunken spree that ended only when the revellers were drenched by a violent rainstorm'.

Early in 1793, just after Arthur Phillip had returned to Britain and left Major Francis Grose temporarily in charge of the fledgling colony, an American ship with the ironic name of the *Hope* sailed into Sydney with a cargo that included 7500 gallons of rum. The captain, one Benjamin Page, refused to sell his cargo except in one lot, including the rum.

The colony had almost starved three years earlier and all supplies were scarce. In light of this and partly to prevent the captain from charging extortionate prices and holding the colony to ransom, the officers of the New South Wales Corps banded together with Grose's blessing to purchase the entire cargo. This gave them a monopoly on rum, which they continued to exploit whenever a new ship arrived in the colony.

Until 1814 rum was the accepted currency in New South Wales. Soldiers were paid in rum, as were convicts who worked on officers' land. According to historian George Mackaness, in 1806 the population of Sydney 'was divided into two classes, those who sold rum and those who drank it'.

This monopoly on land grants, imported goods, meat and rum by the officers of what became known as the Rum Corps led eventually to the corruption that caused the so-called 'Rum Rebellion' of 1808, when the corps successfully rose up against the governor of the day, William Bligh.

Bligh was given the unenviable task of taking control of the twenty-year-old convict colony away from the officers of the New South Wales Corps, especially John Macarthur, and Major George Johnston, who had, along with others like Surgeon-General Thomas Jamison, managed to effectively run the colony to suit themselves, receiving huge land grants and monopolising trade, especially in rum. Previous governors Hunter and King had failed to break the power of the New South Wales Corps and had retired defeated.

The problem was, in part, due to the fact that the governors before Macquarie (Phillip, Hunter, King and Bligh) were naval men—while those in control in the colony were army officers, or ex-officers, who had established themselves as the colony's leading free citizens.

Bligh was a hero in the eyes of the admiralty, having helped win the naval battle of Camperdown off the Dutch coast during the French Revolutionary War. He also defied the mutineers on the *Bounty* and then navigated the ship's launch, in which he and eighteen loyal crew members were set adrift, across 7000 kilometres of open sea to Timor. The journey took them via the island of Tofua, where they were attacked and one man was killed, past Fiji and across the Coral Sea to the coast of northeast Australia, through the Great Barrier Reef and on to Dutch Timor. The launch was designed to hold ten men; the voyage lasted 45 days and all seventeen men made it to Timor.

Although he was seen as a hard man who could take control of the colony and sort out the problems caused by opportunism and monopolies, Bligh had little control over the military and was short-tempered and undiplomatic. He was given direct instructions in London to take the rum trade out of the officers' hands, and he did ban the use of spirits as payment for other goods, and stopped John McArthur importing stills to make rum, but that was only a small part of the power struggle that led to the 'rebellion'.

Bligh stopped land grants, removed military men from the court system and favoured the poorer free settlers who needed help after the Hawkesbury River floods of 1806. Poorer settlers and ex-convicts were being forced to pay high prices for meat and other goods monopolised by the officers of the New South Wales Corps and other large land holders.

In fact, the so-called 'Rum Rebellion' was not called by that name until after 1855 when an English Quaker historian, William Howitt, wrote a history of Australia and exaggerated the 'alcoholic' aspect of the rebellion in order to stress the evils of drink. Howitt invented the term 'Rum Rebellion' and it stuck, which meant other important aspects of the power struggle have been forgotten.

In order to maintain a more usual style of authority, Bligh's successor Lachlan Macquarie arrived with his own regiment in 1810 and the Rum Corps was disbanded. At last the colony had an army man in charge. A canny Scot, Macquarie cleverly established a currency by purchasing a cargo of 10,000 Spanish dollars in 1814 and having the centre cut out of every coin. This had the double purpose of providing two coins of different denominations and rendering the coins useless outside the colony, so the currency remained in New South Wales. This strange coin, known as the 'holey dollar' (the bit in the middle, of less value, was known as the 'dump'), replaced rum as the colony's currency.

Macquarie was to write another chapter in the alcoholic history of New South Wales. In order to further control the rum trade, he gave the monopoly to import the spirit to a group of businessmen. In exchange they built Sydney's first hospital, which still exists. So, Sydney's first major public institution was built in exchange for rum, and was known for years as the Rum Hospital.

There is, of course, no alcoholic history of Australia before 1788, as Aboriginal society had remained grog-free for 60,000 years. The devastating impact of the British invasion on Aboriginal society has been well documented. The clash of two cultures, one with a long social history of drinking and one with no such background, could have only one sad result.

The extreme impact of alcohol on Aboriginal life and culture was noted and lamented within the first years of settlement. Many settlers, as Manning Clark records, were 'appalled by the disastrous effects of civilization on the natives, many of whom became hopeless drunkards, prepared to fight, dance, indeed do anything for the temporary gratification to be obtained from a bottle of rum'.

Sadly alcohol, one of the most devious weapons of the invader, has continued to cause problems for the Aboriginal population for more than two hundred years.

Even though things were not much better back home in Britain, the colony's drinking reputation was well established by 1840, when Archdeacon Henry Jeffreys noted that 'England is becoming the greatest drunkard in the world, except her progeny New South Wales who is said, if it is possible, to drink even deeper still'.

In the first 60 years of European settlement, Australia's population spread well ahead of any authority. Various governors attempted to control this expansion into land that wasn't surveyed or officially owned by the Crown, but it was a losing battle, as was any attempt to regulate or control the production and selling of alcohol in these areas. So the 'shanty' or 'sly grog shop' became the standard drinking establishment of the rural areas of the colony. The quality of the grog offered was dreadful, sometimes fatal, but the climate was hot, the men's work was hard and physical, and women were scarce (indeed, for much of the 19th century, men outnumbered women by four to one), so drinking was the chief recreation after a spell of shearing, droving, fencing, mining or tree cutting.

Although Australians were to become known as great beer drinkers, beer or ale was not the main alcoholic choice until late in the 19th century; it was merely one form of 'grog'. In 1860 a rather frustrated temperance crusader, Nathaniel Pidgeon, noted that 'By a rough calculation, it would appear that one gallon of beer, 1½ pints of brandy, 1¼ pints of gin, and a quart of rum has arrived for every man, woman and child in the colony! It is surely high time for the friends of humanity to bestir themselves!'

'Friends of humanity', however, were not particularly thick upon the ground in most areas of the continent at the time. Indeed, thanks partly to the goldrushes, the kind of friendship that was developing was known as 'mateship', and part of mateship was a very strong dependence on drinking as a bonding and social experience among men.

This anonymous rhyme sums up Australian drinking habits of the time:

> Now Louis likes his native wine and Otto likes his beer,
> The Pommy goes for 'half and half' because it gives him cheer.
> Angus likes his whisky neat and Paddy likes his tot,
> The Aussie has no drink at all—he likes the bloody lot!

With widespread refrigeration and ice production in the 1880s and 1890s, beer became the standard drink for most Australian men, which is, I suppose, not surprising given the climate and the general outdoor style of work at the time. Pubs and shanties needed refrigeration to attract customers from about 1890, such was the popularity of a cold beer. Ever since then, Aussies have loved a 'coldie'.

———

While trying to locate the oldest pub in Australia is surprisingly difficult (it depends on what criteria you use and the whole problem is dealt with elsewhere in this collection), there is no such doubt about the oldest brewery in Australia.

Our oldest brewery is the now-famous Cascade Brewery in South Hobart, which began in 1832 and is still going strong today.

An amazing character, Englishman Peter Degraves, received permission to build the brewery in 1824 but the business wasn't established for another eight years. The reason it took so long was that Degraves was in prison!

Peter Degraves was born in 1778, in Dover, into a well-respected family of French descent. His father was a doctor and Peter studied engineering. He was a risk taker who was imprisoned for theft and was bankrupt for several years before deciding to emigrate to Van Diemen's Land in 1821 with his family and his brother-in-law and business partner, Major Hugh McIntosh.

They purchased a ship called the *Hope* (coincidentally the same name as the ship that brought the first cargo of rum to Sydney in 1793) and raised money for the venture by selling passages to migrants.

Degraves was arrested for overcrowding the ship and then imprisoned for debt, but finally arrived in Hobart with his wife and eight children in 1824. In their first year, he and McIntosh were granted land at the Cascades, and started a sawmilling business as well as providing water to Hobart from a dam they built.

In 1826 his creditors in Britain renewed charges against Degraves and he was imprisoned and faced bankruptcy again when a British judge decided the discharge of the previous debt was not valid in law. Degraves was in custody until 1831 when Governor Arthur had him released. While in Hobart Prison, he designed new plans for remodelling it.

The court took the sawmill and his house but, after Degraves' release, he and McIntosh soon started a second sawmill, a flour mill and several bake houses, as well as the brewery, which they built in 1832. It was reputed that the beer, timber, flour, bread and biscuits they produced brought in about £100,000 a year.

Water rights for the brewery were a problem and, when the government built a dam above Degraves' water source in the 1840s, he attempted to sue the Public Works Department. When the editor of the *Hobart Town Guardian* criticised him, Degraves threatened the newspaperman—and was prosecuted and briefly imprisoned again in 1848 for doing so. He eventually lost his battle over water rights.

Meanwhile, Degraves' business empire had continued to grow in various directions. In 1834 he had formed a syndicate that designed and built the Theatre Royal, renowned as the best theatre in Australia. After a disagreement with the other syndicate members, Degraves became the sole proprietor in 1841.

After McIntosh died in 1835, Degraves started a shipbuilding business and built many large ships, including the barque *Tasman*; at 563 tons, she was the biggest vessel built in Van Diemen's Land at the time. When the goldrush began in Victoria, he loaded his ships with timber, which was used to build thousands of houses in the rapidly growing 'town' of Melbourne.

Degraves died at Hobart on 31 December 1852, but he lives on in two of his achievements: the Theatre Royal still stands today, almost unchanged from when it was built, the oldest theatre in Australia; and famous Cascade beer, 'from the clear waters of Tasmania', is still just about the best drop you can drink!

Cascade may be among Australia's oldest beers, but which is the most Australian?

In the 1970s and 1980s you may well have heard the phrase 'as Aussie as Foster's lager' in Britain and the USA especially, where

Foster's was marketed as the beer Aussies made and loved to drink. The slogan for Foster's was 'It's Australian for *beer*'.

Well, it may have been marketed as 'Australian for *beer*', but what *is* the answer to the question, 'How Aussie is Foster's?'

If you take the nationality of the founders of Foster's famous beer into account, it's not Aussie at all—it's American!

The Foster brothers, Ralph and William, arrived in Melbourne in 1887 and they were not primarily interested in beer or brewing. They were middle-aged entrepreneurs who set themselves up as pioneers in the refrigeration industry and only made beer in order to demonstrate the wonders of refrigeration. The Fosters arrived with the latest refrigeration equipment, set up their brewery and, in 1888, successfully made the first local 'lager style' beer in Australia, a beer that needed to be kept cold to be enjoyed properly.

Having done what they had planned to do, Ralph and William promptly sold their entire enterprise to some locals in 1889.

It appears there may have been some urgency about the need to sell and skedaddle on Ralph's part. The *Melbourne Argus* reported, on 8 February 1888, that Ralph Rose Foster of Fitzroy had appeared in the Insolvency Court, having left St Louis owing over $200,000.

It seems that some very shady past deals had caught up with Ralph, who left Melbourne in 1889 and wound up in Italy, where he applied for a US passport in 1895. Younger brother William moved to Double Bay in Sydney with his wife and young son and died aged 46 in 1891, ironically, some may think, of cirrhosis of the liver. His wife, Annie, died in 1903.

Their son, also William, who was twenty when his mother died, spent his life as a teacher in outback New South Wales and died in 1953. His great-granddaughters Karyn and Tracey, who kindly provided me with the family information used here, say that Ralph was the black sheep of the family and could even be called 'the Christopher Skase of his day'.

———

In 1908 there was a massive amalgamation of breweries in Melbourne. Carlton, McCracken's City, Castlemaine, Shamrock and Foster's breweries all combined to form Carlton United, and the Foster's brewery in Rokeby Street was closed and the Foster's name almost lost. Carlton United only continued to brew a beer branded as 'Foster's' because there was some demand for the label in Queensland and Western Australia.

Its revival began in 1971 when Foster's was introduced to England through Barry Humphries' highly successful cartoon strip in the magazine *Private Eye*. The strip was used as the basis for two very successful movies, *The Adventures of Barry McKenzie* and *Barry McKenzie Holds His Own*. The hero of the cartoon strip and movies was rarely seen without a can of Foster's in his hand and Foster's took off in Britain, where cold, lager-style beer was just taking over the beer market from the more traditional styles.

Foster's then launched into the USA in 1972, where it was marketed along with sport. Foster's sponsored the 1974 America's Cup challenge and was the official Olympic beer for Australia at the 1984 Los Angeles Olympics.

For more than a decade from 1985, the Melbourne Cup was known as the Foster's Melbourne Cup. Then Paul Hogan was brought in to the advertising campaign.

Hoges' first Foster's commercial script read:

> G'day. They've asked me over from Oz to introduce youse all to Foster's Draught, here it is. Cripes! I'd better start with the basics. It's a light, golden liquid, except for the white bit on top, the head, and it's brewed from malt, yeast and hops. Technical term is Lager. That's L-A-G-E-R. But everyone calls it Foster's. Ahhhh, ripper! Tastes like an angel cryin' on yer tongue. Foster's.

Of course, the famous 'Aussie Foster's Lager' marketed to Poms and Yanks was also brewed there—not here in Australia. Foster's is brewed in eight countries, including China, Spain and Sweden! It is sold in 135 countries.

Us Aussies living in Britain and the United States in the 1980s spent a lot of our time telling the locals we didn't drink Foster's at home. After all, it was an American invention!

The formation of Carlton United Breweries in 1908 created a massive company with economies of scale unmatched by any other brewer in Australia. Their famous ad featured an old bushie at the bar saying, 'I allus has wan at eleven.'

Castlemaine Brewery had been founded by the two Fitzgerald brothers. They migrated from Galway, Ireland, in 1859 and began their brewing business at Castlemaine in Victoria. In 1875 they established a brewery in South Melbourne and, in 1877, they also set up in Brisbane from where they brewed the famous Castlemaine Ale that became associated with Queensland—although it was named after a town in Victoria!

The beer became Castlemaine XXXX in 1916 and ever since that time the joke has been that it's called XXXX because Queenslanders can't spell 'beer'.

If you're wondering what 'four X' was called before 1916 . . . cease wondering. From 1878 to 1916 it was called 'Castlemaine XXX Sparkling Ale'—in other words 'three X'!

———

While 20th century Australia remained basically a beer-drinking nation, all the alcoholic trends that developed in other Western countries were also experienced here. Cocktail drinking became trendy and popular in the 1920s and 1930s, and awareness of more sophisticated food and wine consumption developed slowly after World War II. New 'boutique' beers and fruit drinks became fads in the 1980s, and their popularity has continued to grow.

Rum remained a popular drink, perhaps partly because of tradition and partly because of the sugar industry that developed in Queensland from the 1860s. Brandy, whisky and gin were also popular, particularly among the middle classes, and there was sherry for the ladies. While toleration of alcoholic excess was the norm among men, it was, after those early riotous years of the colonies, rarely extended to women.

Grapevines were one of the first crops grown in the colony and regions like the Hunter Valley have a long and praiseworthy history of producing great wines from the earliest days of settlement. In South Australia, German migrants and other pioneer families had established a tradition of fine wine production by the late 19th century in areas like Barossa, Clare, McLaren Vale and Langhorne Creek.

But general appreciation of wine did not really come to Australia until the 1980s, when the wine industry took off. Its spectacular growth coincided with a changing attitude to drinking generally. Australia had slipped well down the table of beer drinkers, from number one in the world for consumption per head of population in the 1950s, to a miserable tenth by 2000.

Although the Australian character, as I said at the start, is often perceived to be 'easy-going' and 'fond of a drink', this has been offset and counterbalanced by some very conservative trends in our social history, tendencies such as 'wowserism', racism and prudery.

Changes in licensing laws have greatly affected drinking habits in Australia. Until 1916 the accepted pub closing time in most states was 11 p.m. However, from 1916 pubs were forced to close at 6 p.m., after state referenda took place in response to the campaign run by the temperance movement and supporters of supposed 'wartime austerity'. This law stayed in place in some states for more than 50 years. The idea was that early closing would improve family life and encourage temperance. What resulted, of course, was the notorious 'six o'clock swill'. Voting in the referenda was heavily influenced by the infamous soldiers' riot that occurred on Valentine's Day 1916 in Sydney. That story is told later in this collection.

Early closing simply led to men drinking as much as they could as fast as they could from the time they finished work until six every evening. Long before its eventual demise, 6 p.m. closing had established a tradition of a regular 'drinking session' in the evenings after work.

Six o'clock closing was abandoned in Tasmania in 1937, and New South Wales changed to ten o'clock closing in 1955. Victoria waited until 1966 and South Australia finally fell into line with other states in 1967, thanks to Don Dunstan, who was keen to shed that state's 'wowser' tag.

Today, Australia is a complex society with different drinking cultures. Many changes have occurred in recent times. We tend to drink more often *with* meals than before or after them as we did in the past. We drink more wine and less beer. We are perhaps more temperate due to strict drink-driving laws and a growing awareness of the harmful effects of alcohol on our health and our society. On the other hand, many Australians are drinking at a younger age, and binge drinking and alcohol abuse are more discussed and worried over than ever.

Attitudes to drinking in our society vary from total acceptance to extreme intolerance. Visitors to our shores have had mixed reactions to our drinking habits. In 1873 English author Anthony Trollope found our drunkenness to be a reflection of some of our better characteristics. 'Australian drunkenness,' he said, 'so far as it exists, is not of the English type. It is more reckless, more extravagant, more riotous, to the imagination of man infinitely more magnificent; but it is less enduring, and certainly upon the whole less debasing.'

A century later, however, in 1975, Danish journalist Poul Nielsen was moved to comment, 'I have felt scared since I arrived in Sydney, in fact I feel more relaxed in New York than here. There is something desperate about the way people drink here.' If he thought that of Sydney, I wonder what he would have made of Darwin.

Perhaps the disparity in opinion has something to with the nationality of the observer. Or perhaps it has more to do with the company Trollope and Nielsen kept while visiting our shores, or with social changes over the intervening century.

Contradictory opinions have always existed on the home front, too. In the year 1974, for instance, an article appeared in the *Australian Church Record* describing the evils of drink inflicted on eleven-year-olds in state schools: 'The girls had their first cooking lesson. The tasty morsel to be cooked was rum balls. Whether rum essence or the real jungle juice scarcely matters. Small girls were to be introduced to this highly desirable alcoholic flavour. Perhaps it is part of the modern approach to cooking, which is to saturate almost everything in some form of alcohol and give it a French name.'

In the same year, advertising agency executive John Singleton commented quite matter-of-factly that 'The advertising industry lives a very cyclical sort of life. December is the month for getting pissed.'

John Singleton is famous for his often-criticised advertising campaigns linking alcohol to 'ockerism' and sport, but drinking and sport have been linked in our history since the earliest colonial times.

Colonial sporting events were often organised by publicans in order to boost sales. Horseracing, foot racing, cycling, boxing, wrestling, cock fighting and various novelty events were used to attract crowds to the field beside the pub. Or, in the case of races, the finish line was at the pub!

Sydney's first *official* horseracing meeting started a trend when it caused widespread drinking and became a three-day holiday for the entire colony. On 15 October 1810, officers of the 73rd Regiment organised a three-day race meeting in Hyde Park. Of course, there had been unofficial meetings before that—often at pubs in outlying areas.

The records tell us that Captain Ritchie's grey gelding Chase won the first official race. The horses raced clockwise as the course design suited that direction due to the position of the sun in the afternoons. The finishing line was where Market Street meets Elizabeth Street today.

The three-day meeting caused massive drinking and rowdiness, and a stray dog brought down D'Arcy Wentworth's good horse, Gig, during a race on the final day. The jockey, incidentally, was D'Arcy's nineteen-year-old son, William Charles Wentworth, who, luckily uninjured in the fall, went on to become one of our greatest and most famous political activists and statesmen.

All in all, the 1810 meeting was deemed to be a huge success and it became a part of the Sydney social calendar until 1814, when the 73rd Regiment was transferred to Ceylon and the colony lost its race committee. But the legacy of those Hyde Park meetings continues today in the many carnivals held throughout Australia where alcohol and horseracing are enjoyed together.

Champagne and rum drinking were common at race meetings, and still are to a certain degree, but since refrigeration came along in the late 1880s, beer and most sports just seem to go together quite naturally in Australia.

There is, of course, a darker side to combining sport, crowds and drinking, and even in the latter half of the 19th century, alcohol-fuelled riots were not uncommon at football matches in Melbourne. The gentle game of cricket, which stops for lunch and tea breaks, is now perhaps the worst example of sport and booze being mixed unwisely by large groups of spectators.

Journalist Rory Gibson once wrote of a match he remembered from the 1970s, when cans were still allowed at major grounds like the Gabba in Brisbane. Apparently a poor Pom paraded on the hill with a huge Union Jack draped around his shoulders. Of course, all the Aussies immediately began using him for target practice and hundreds of beer cans rained down from further up the hill. He attempted to run but that was only further incentive for the locals to pick up the thousands of 'empties' lying around and pelt them at him.

When he eventually crouched down and covered his head with his hands, a very unsympathetic Aussie fan picked up one of the 44-gallon-drum garbage tins full of empties and poured the lot over him. The crowd cheered as the police arrived and the poor Pom was arrested for 'inciting the crowd'.

Evidently he was led away smiling and everyone was happy—just another day at the cricket.

Sponsorship of sport by alcohol companies has become a serious business. Rory Gibson reminds us that former North Queensland Cowboys rugby league player Ian Russell was twice fined by his club, for $5000 and then $10,000, for being seen by team officials publicly drinking a can of VB, when the team was sponsored by XXXX. That's an expensive can of beer!

The famous competition between Foster's and Lion Nathan for Spring Racing Carnival sponsorship rights in Melbourne is another example of the importance of booze in the world of sport.

Wendy Green, the Darwin school teacher whose horse, Rogan Josh, won the 1999 Melbourne Cup, tells a great yarn about driving back to Darwin after the Cup and stopping at Tennant Creek to celebrate with some locals who were having a party. She was recognised and soon joined the festivities, which became a celebration of her Cup win.

Towards the end of the celebration, a local mum asked Wendy to christen her new baby boy. She wanted to call him 'Rogan Josh'. When Wendy asked the mother if she was sure about the name, she was told that it was fine, in fact it was almost traditional as there was another distant relative from the same Aboriginal tribe who had been christened 'Phar Lap Dixon'.

Wendy explained that she wasn't qualified and joked that she had no holy water handy. She suggested that the captain of a tourist bus which had pulled in to join the fun might be qualified in the same way as a ship's captain. The bus driver was reluctant but agreed to do the job, no doubt realising he'd be a thousand miles away in two days' time!

So they were set to christen baby Rogan Josh, but when the mum offered a can of VB to be used instead of holy water, Wendy protested. She pointed out that Foster's was the official sponsor of the Melbourne Cup and it didn't seem right. So she offered the French champagne she had in her car and everyone was happy with that.

———

How does the average Australian handle the contradictory views of disapproval and acceptance of alcohol? How do we cope with attempts to restrict and control our drinking and yet remain true to the Aussie belief in a 'fair go'? Perhaps some insight can be gained from this item which appeared a few years ago in the

*Sydney Morning Herald*'s Column 8: 'By chance a colleague booked into a north Queensland motel before learning that its dining-room was not licensed. "Think nothing of it," said the waitress. "If you want a bottle of beer with your steak, just say Steak and Laundry. It doesn't show on the records."'

# I ALLUS HAS WAN AT ELEVEN

## Anonymous

> I allus has wan at eleven,
> It's a duty that has to be done.
> If I *don't* have wan at eleven
> I *must* have eleven at wan.

The first line of this poem, 'I allus has wan at eleven' ('I always have one at eleven'), was used for decades on posters and signs advertising Carlton United beer. The ad showed a genial old bearded bushman standing at a bar with his beer.

# ONE HUNDRED STUBBIES

**Kenneth Cook**

> 'The stubbie is one of the most malevolent inventions of the decade.'
>
> Bishop Shevill, Anglican bishop of
> North Queensland, 1970

To understand how this could happen, you have to know something about where it happened—Coober Pedy, an almost impossible town in the arid centre. Coober Pedy is an opal-mining town. The name is Aboriginal for 'white man in a hole'. The 'hole' refers to the mines and to the houses, which are caves dug into the sides of low hills. In the summer the temperature averages around 50 degrees Celsius. You spend most of your time underground or in a pub, or you die.

I had driven up from Adelaide in an air-conditioned car and I thought I was going to die.

I saw Coober Pedy in the distance as thousands of tiny round bubbles in the shimmering desert heat haze. Soon these bubbles resolved themselves into the waste piles from the opal mines that stretch endlessly out from the town in all directions.

The whole area looks as though it is infested by the termites that build those huge nests of mud. Many of the mines are deserted and local legend has it that they contain the bones of reckless men who have welshed on gambling debts or tried robbing mines. I never actually heard of a skeleton being found.

The sight of the pub in Coober Pedy automatically brought my car to a halt. I needed cold beer, and lots of it. The heat out there is almost solid and you can feel it dropping on your head when you step out of the car. I trotted across to the pub, my whole being yearning for beer, totally unaware that I was about to witness an event that would put me off beer drinking for months.

The pub was moderately full of pink men. Almost all the men in Coober Pedy are pink because they are opal miners and the pink dust of the mines becomes ingrained in their skins. Or perhaps they never wash, because the water there is pretty foul stuff.

I ordered beer, found it deliciously cold as beer always is in outback Australia, often the only evidence of any form of civilised living, and began tuning in to the talk around me, as is my habit.

Two pink men quite near me were having a conversation which was absurd, like most conversations in outback pubs by the time everyone has had five beers. The two of them were leaning on the bar, peering earnestly into each other's deep-etched faces. Like two grotesque dolls, they carried on a nonsensical argument.

'He can.'

'It'd kill him.'

'It'd take four hours.'

'It wouldn't kill him. Nothing would.'

I leaned closer. Their voices were beginning to hit an hysterical note. Like buzzsaws, their shouts rose above the hubbub of the other drinkers. They were obviously used to yelling at one another fifteen metres underground with jackhammers going full blast.

'A hundred stubbies in four hours. Do you reckon that would kill him?'

'It'd kill anybody.'

'He's not anybody.'

They stared into each other's faces, the importance of the topic growing in their minds as the beer ran down their throats.

'Why are you so bloody sure?'

'Because I'm bloody sure.'

One of them was almost middle-aged, with grey hair all over his exposed shoulders. At least, it would have been grey if he had washed off the pink dust. His face was dulled and brutalised by years of grubbing away in the ground all morning and drinking beer all afternoon. Or perhaps he had been born with a dull and brutal face.

His companion was younger, probably not thirty, a little fat but with the heavy shoulders and arm muscles of the opal digger. If men keep on digging in the ground for opal for a few generations, they will probably develop forequarters and arms like wombats. This younger man looked like a hairy-nosed wombat because of the three-day growth on his face. Not exactly like a wombat, though, because a wombat has some expression on its face if you look hard enough, while this character's face was just a blob of pendulous blankness. With its pink-dusted stubble, it looked like a discarded serving of blancmange growing a strange mould.

'Well, if you're sure, will you bet on it?'

'Sure I'll bet on it.'

You couldn't tell who was speaking because their voices sounded identical, like knives scraping on plates at an unbearably high volume. But you could tell the sound was coming from them and gradually a pool of silence was forming around them as the rest of the bar tuned in to their conversation.

'What do you reckon, Ivan?'

Now you could see who was speaking because the older man turned and addressed himself to the drinker alongside him.

Ivan turned slowly and I realised I was looking at a monster. He stood barely a metre and a half high and was almost as wide across the shoulders. His chest, black-singleted and covered with dust, stood out like a giant cockerel's, a vast billow of muscles with dark streaks running over the pink dust as the sweat made its own little rivers. One great arm hung disproportionately low by his side, the other rested on the bar with an enormous pink hand almost totally concealing a glass of beer. His hair was short and closely cropped and he carried a comb of bristles over a face that for one mad moment made me wonder whether it is possible to cross a crocodile with a hippopotamus.

This was a face that displayed a complete lack of interest and malice, with a blank complacency that made it obvious no thought had ever disturbed the brain that nestled just under that absurd cockscomb of hair.

He was wearing shorts, and two massive legs, not unlike those of a hippopotamus except that they were pink and hairy instead of grey and wrinkly, propped up his body. It was as though the body was resting on the legs rather than being joined to them, because he seemed to have no waist; he was tree-trunk-thick all the way down until suddenly he had legs. The junction was concealed by the baggy shorts, but I got the impression that the legs might walk away at any moment, leaving the body standing there.

'What do you reckon, Ivan? I reckon you could drink a hundred stubbies in four hours.'

''Course I could,' said Ivan. His voice was flat and deep, almost pleasant by comparison with those of the other two, but only by comparison.

'There,' said the older man, turning to his companion as though everything had been proven.

'Bet you he couldn't.'

'Bet then. Go on, bet!'

'What do you mean, bet?'

'I mean what I say. What'll you bet he can't drink a hundred stubbies in four hours?'

'Bet you five hundred bucks.'

The older man thrust his hand into his hip pocket and brought out a wad of notes. He counted ten fifties on to the counter. The younger man looked on impassively while Ivan, losing interest, turned back to his pint.

'Match that.'

The younger man, having waited until the last fifty was laid down, dived into his own pocket and counted out his bundle of fifties. He paused before laying down the tenth.

'Who's paying for the beer?' he asked cunningly.

There was a long pause while this was pondered.

'Take it out of the centre,' said the older man at last.

'All right, Ivan. Here's the biggest beer-up of your life, and on me,' said the older man, grabbing Ivan by the shoulder. 'Come on, Bill,' he said to the barman, 'set up ten stubbies. Ivan's gonna sink a hundred.'

Bill didn't react, just reached into the refrigerator and lined ten stubbies up on the counter.

'Off you go, Ivan. Remember, I'm betting on you.'

'He's gotta be standing at the end,' said the younger man, sullenly, now sounding worried.

'He'll be standing. Come on, Ivan. Sink 'em.'

Ivan was looking at the ten stubbies. You could see he was thinking by the contortions on his face. You could almost hear him. The three men were now the centre of a large circle that had formed as the concept of the bizarre bet was grasped by the other drinkers. Money was appearing from dusty pockets as side bets were laid. Ivan was still thinking.

'Come on, Ivan.'

'I want a hundred bucks,' said Ivan.

The older man was shocked. 'What do you mean, you want a hundred bucks?'

'I mean I want a hundred bucks.'

'Whaffor?'

'Drinking the beer.'

'But you're getting the beer free.'

'I want a hundred bucks.' Conversations tend to be limited on the opal fields.

'You can go to hell.'

'Right.'

Ivan turned back to the bar and ordered another beer. The older man looked at this disbelievingly. Ivan downed his beer. Obviously he intended to stand by his position.

'All right then,' said the older man desperately, 'if you drink all of the hundred stubbies, I'll give you a hundred bucks.'

'A hundred for trying,' returned Ivan, without even turning around.

'God Almighty. What happens if you drink fifty beers and pack it in? Do I still give you a hundred dollars?'

'A hundred for trying,' said Ivan.

The older man stared at the impossibly broad and unyielding back. You could tell that he was thinking, struggling for a solution. 'Tell you what,' he said finally, 'a hundred and fifty if you make it, nothing if you don't. How's that?'

Ivan was thinking. A long pause. 'All right,' he said, and reached for the first stubbie.

'Take if off the top,' said the older man to his companion, which presumably meant that the winner would have to pay Ivan's fee.

This seemed reasonable to the younger man, but he was slow to make up his mind. By the time he had nodded assent, Ivan had already drunk six stubbies.

His technique was impressive. He picked up one of the little squat bottles in each hand and flicked the tops off with his thumbs. Most men need a metal implement for this, but not Ivan—he had thumbnails he could use as chisels. Then he raised his right hand, threw back his head and poured the beer into his gaping mouth all at once, the whole bottleful, one continuous little jet of beer until the bottle was empty. Then he did the same with the bottle in his left hand. Both bottles empty, he put them down neatly on the counter and reached for two more.

There are 375 millilitres of beer in each of these bottles. Legally, if you drink three in an hour, you are too drunk to drive a motor car. One hundred bottles would be 37,500 millilitres. The mathematics are beyond me, but it must be a monumental weight of beer. I timed him. It took just on eight seconds to empty a bottle, one second to put the two bottles on the counter, one second to pick up two more, one second to flip off the tops. He was swallowing a stubbie every eleven seconds.

Swallowing's not the word. There was no movement in his throat. He was just pouring it straight down into his stomach. A stubbie every eleven seconds. At that rate, he would be able to drink 100 in 1100 seconds—that's less than an hour. But he couldn't keep that up. For obvious reasons; he'd burst, for one.

I wasn't the only man in the bar making these calculations. In the great circle that now surrounded Ivan, men were looking at their watches and counting. To save time the barman had put twenty cold stubbies on the counter just as Ivan downed the tenth. Ivan didn't pause. He was drinking, or working, as rhythmically as though he were on an assembly line: pour down one bottle, pour down the next, both bottles on the counter, pick up the next two, flip off the tops, pour down one bottle, pour down the next.

The only sound in the bar was the slap of the bottles on the counter and the metallic rattle of the bottle tops hitting the floor. All the drinkers were silent, watching in an almost religious awe, their own glasses held unnoticed.

I realised for the first time that the clock hanging above the bottles at the back of the bar had a chime. It chimed six o'clock just as Ivan finished his fortieth bottle of beer. As if it were a signal, he slammed the two bottles on the bar and paused. The silence became intense as everybody started leaning forward slightly, wondering. I was convinced Ivan would drop dead.

Ivan stood motionless, his hands on the bar, his body inclined slightly forward. The pause lengthened, the silence deepened, if silence can deepen. I could even hear the clock ticking. Suddenly, Ivan's back muscles convulsed and a monumental belch erupted through the bar, breaking the silence like a violent crack of thunder. I swear the front rank of spectators reeled back. There was a burst of cheering and laughing and clapping.

Ivan reached for the next two bottles and was back to his rhythm again. Forty-five bottles, fifty, fifty-five, sixty. The impossible was being translated into reality in front of our eyes. Then came a piece of virtuosity: Ivan flipped the tops off two bottles but instead of raising his right hand, he raised both hands and poured the contents of two bottles down his throat simultaneously. It took just eight seconds. Seven hundred and fifty millilitres of beer in eight seconds to join the flood that was already coursing through his stomach, intestines, bloodstream.

Technically he had to be dead. No human tissue could withstand an assault of alcohol like that. Perhaps Ivan wasn't human; perhaps he had never been alive. He had stopped again. He glanced around the circle of spectators.

'Had it, Ivan?' said one hopefully.

Ivan ignored him.

He looked to his principal, the older drinker. There was some-thing he'd forgotten, a condition in the contract that hadn't been spelled out.

'Time out to leak?' he said, a little plaintively.

'Sure, get going,' said his backer.

Ivan was away from the bar for five minutes, which wasn't surprising. I wondered whether he had regurgitated some of the beer, but this didn't seem to occur to anybody else.

At eighty bottles, Ivan stopped again. We waited expectantly for the mighty belch, but it didn't come. He paused for about fifteen seconds and then reached for two new bottles. But there was a change of pace. The mighty fingernails fumbled slightly before the bottle tops flew off. His movements were deliberate and ponderous. Once he missed his aim and a jet of beer splashed onto his chin. I wondered whether this counted as a whole bottle but nobody raised the point. He was pausing each time he set down the bottles.

I was aware that gently, almost whispering, the whole bar was counting: 'Eighty-five, eighty-six, eighty-seven, eighty-eight.' The count was slowing as Ivan's drinking rate slowed. By now he was taking fifteen seconds a bottle, then eighteen, nineteen. At ninety-five bottles, Ivan stopped again, one half-full bottle in his left hand. He leaned forward. We waited again for the belch, but there was no sound.

Ivan shook his head from side to side. I saw his eyes. They had gone completely white, like a blind man's. Ivan started to sway.

'Come on, Ivan, into 'em, boy!'

Ivan's massive body swung around in a slow circle, his feet still firmly on the floor. But then he steadied himself and the giant hand was raised. But this time he put the bottle to his lips. It did not go down in one unbroken stream. He swallowed many times with great effort. He put the bottle on the counter and reached for two more. He couldn't get the tops off; the barman whipped them off for him. Slowly, painfully, his eyeballs rolled deep into his head, his body swaying in ever-increasing circles, Ivan drank each bottle.

'Ninety-nine!' It was a roar.

Then Ivan drank the ninety-ninth bottle. By then he was spinning quickly, inclining his body at an impossible angle. Only the weight and size of his legs can have kept him upright.

Somebody had to put the hundredth bottle into his hand. Obviously he couldn't see it, or anything else for that matter, but somehow his hand found his gyrating head and he got the bottle to his lips.

Down went the beer, slowly, terribly slowly. But down it went, all of it.

'One hundred!' It was a mighty animal scream. The empty bottle crashed to the floor. Ivan had drunk one hundred stubbies in just under an hour.

Three or four men tried to stop Ivan spinning and there was a general hubbub as bets were settled and fresh drinks ordered. Then Ivan brought instant silence with a vast bellow.

'Vodka!' he shouted.

The word, as much as the level of Ivan's thunderous voice, brought the silence.

He turned to the bar and thumped it.

'Vodka!'

Dazed, the barman poured him a nip of vodka.

Ivan brushed the glass off the bar with a sweep of his hand that demolished half a dozen other drinkers' glasses as well.

'The bottle!' he roared.

There was silence.

Then, timidly, terrified in the presence of mystical greatness, the barman put a bottle of vodka on the counter. It was open, but Ivan broke its neck on the bar in a ritual gesture. Apparently he could see again, although his eyes were still just blank white.

He raised the vodka bottle until the jagged neck was a handspan from his mouth, then poured a gush of the clear spirit down his throat. Half the bottle gone, he slapped it down on the counter; it rolled on its side and the vodka slopped onto the floor. Nobody noticed.

Arms by his side, eyes pure white, body rigid, Ivan made for the door of the bar. A quick passage cleared for him and he went through in a stumbling rush, like a train through a forest. He crashed into the swinging door, the bright flash of late sunlight illuminating his huge frame, and plunged headfirst out into the street, hitting the dust with a thud that seemed to shake the building. Just once his head moved, and then he was a motionless heap of sweat-sodden humanity in the dust.

'We'd better get a truck to take the poor bastard home,' said somebody.

'Yeah.' And two of the drinkers, kindly men, wandered off to organise the truck.

'He's forgotten his money,' said someone else.

'I'll keep it for him,' said the barman. 'He'll be back in the morning. Probably have a head.'

# THE FELLOW FROM SYDNEY

**Anonymous**

There was a young fellow from Sydney
Who drank till he ruined his kidney.
It shrivelled and shrank
As he sat there and drank,
But he had a good time at it, didn't he?

# THE MAN WHO STOLE NINE CHOOKS . . . AND WAS GIVEN A COW

**Jim Haynes**

> 'Ye who wish to lie here, drink Squire's beer.'
>
> Reported as an epitaph on a tombstone
> in a Parramatta churchyard by naval surgeon
> Peter Cunningham, c.1827

The name James Squire is a famous and popular one in Australia today, as a brand name for a range of beers, but just who was James Squire?

He is remembered and revered by many Australians as the first man to grow hops and brew beer commercially in the colony of New South Wales. Apart from that, most Australians know nothing about his story, which is a shame because it is a remarkable and fascinating yarn.

Transported on the First Fleet to serve seven years for stealing, James Squire had an unusual background. He was from a family of gypsies; in fact, his parents were from the two Romany families involved in one of Britain's most scandalous court cases, the Canning Case, in which public outrage and prejudice against gypsies, or Romanies, or 'Egyptians' as they were dubbed, caused a major miscarriage of justice in 1754.

Squire's maternal grandmother, Susannah Wells, was convicted of abducting a young domestic servant, Elizabeth Canning, and keeping her imprisoned for a month. His other grandmother,

Mary Squire, was also accused of taking part in the assault and the theft of Elizabeth Canning's corsets, which Mary Squire was alleged to have 'forcibly removed'.

Susannah Wells was found guilty, branded on the arm and imprisoned, but she was later exonerated when the maid, Elizabeth Canning, was convicted of perjury. Mary Squire was sentenced to death for allegedly stealing the corsets, but later pardoned.

As a Romany, or gypsy, Squire grew up to a life of crime as a fringe dweller, smuggling and stealing. Romanies were feared and persecuted and denied civil rights in 18th century Britain. They did, however, have good knowledge of hop cultivation as they provided the itinerant workforce for the hop planting and picking.

The transformation of James Squire from a despised criminal from the lowest social rank imaginable in England to a respectable and revered citizen of Sydney is an amazing story. It shows how the convict system could achieve amazing social reform by simply putting people in a place where their past was irrelevant to what they might achieve.

Squire was lucky to be alive to be sent to New South Wales. He had been found guilty previously of highway robbery after he ran from a house he had broken in to and was arrested. The sentence, if he had been arrested inside the house, was death. He was sentenced to transportation to the American colonies but served the sentence in the army instead, and was running a tavern at Kingston near London when he was found guilty of stealing nine chooks. The tavern he ran was, by all accounts, a den of thieves, smugglers, prostitutes and gypsies.

For stealing nine chooks, James Squire was transported on the First Fleet to what was to become a totally different life in New South Wales.

Old habits die hard, though. It took a while before James Squire, gypsy and thief, was able to transform himself into Mr James Squire, esquire, respectable and successful businessman, philanthropist and local constable.

In March 1789, Squire was sentenced to 150 lashes for the theft of medical supplies from Surgeon John White's store. It is not certain that the full sentence was ever carried out. He claimed at the time the herb he stole, 'horehound', was a tonic for his pregnant girlfriend, the convict Mary Spencer. As a drug the plant was often used to relieve pain and discomfort during pregnancy. Squire admitted years later that he stole the herb because it was a substitute for hops in the brewing process.

Squire had been making beer and selling it at four pence a quart to the officers of the New South Wales Corps since the establishment of the colony.

His punishment was a slight one in the circumstances; normally such a theft was punished by hanging. No doubt the fact that he was already supplying beer to the officers had some effect on the leniency of the sentence.

When Mary Spencer gave birth to a son, Francis, in 1791, James, aware that he could not support a child, enlisted him in the New South Wales Corps as an infant and he went on the payroll on his seventh birthday—as a drummer boy.

James Squire was a paradox as far as caring for his offspring was concerned. He left a wife and three children behind in England and fathered another eight in Sydney, seven of them with his second mistress, his convict servant Sarah Mason.

His cunning Romany ways were apparent in his land dealings. He added twelve other land grants to his own 30 acres (12 hectares) at Ryde and eventually had an estate of more than 800 acres (325 hectares) along the Parramatta River. He cleverly complained to the Colonial Secretary about neighbouring land grants not being taken up and consequently purchased several of them for a shilling each.

Squire cultivated hops and grain and was the first successful brewer in Australia. He obtained a licence to sell liquor in partnership with another emancipist, Simeon Lord, in 1792, and set up the Malting Shovel Tavern on the river at Kissing Point, near Ryde. It was at the halfway point on the river between the two settlements of Sydney and Parramatta and proved a great success.

Oddly enough, the brewing of beer was seen as a good thing for a colony that was corrupted by the trade in rum. Rum had become the currency of the colony and led to a rebellion and massive military corruption.

It was considered a sobering influence to get the inhabitants of New South Wales to drink beer rather than rum, and Squire was much praised for his efforts in growing hops and grain and producing and selling a decent brew. Beer was actually considered to be a healthy and efficacious beverage!

This belief was partly due to the fact that 'small beer', very mildly alcoholic beer (less than 1 per cent), was universally consumed in parts of Europe, especially Northern Europe and the 'low countries', throughout medieval times and into the 17th and 18th centuries. Small beer was brewed in most households for consumption by workers, children and servants because water sources were polluted and the brewing process meant small beer was a safer way to quench the thirst. It was common for men doing heavy manual labour in hot weather to consume six litres or more a day of 'small beer'.

James Squire was a very canny businessman with a gypsy's nose for horse-trading, but what I like about him is his egalitarian spirit and support of the underdog, which I have no doubt came from his Romany background. Squire set up a credit union for emancipated convicts and helped many less fortunate than himself. He was a friend to the Aborigines and especially to Bennelong, the Aboriginal who was befriended by Governor Phillip and had been to Britain and back.

When Bennelong fell on hard times later in life, he spent much of his time on Squire's farm and he was buried there, with a memorial erected by Squire.

The noted artist (and forger) Joseph Lycett said of him, 'Had he not been so generous, James Squire would have been a much wealthier man ... his name will long be pronounced with veneration by the grateful objects of his liberality.'

Squire was an industrious and successful farmer. One hop vine he cultivated in 1806 covered 5 acres (2 hectares) by 1812 and produced 700 kilograms of hops. As a brewer he was similarly successful; by 1820 his brewery was producing 40 hogsheads (about 10,000 litres) of beer a week.

When he died in 1822, his funeral was the largest ever seen in the colony up to that time. His grandson, James Squire Farnell, would be premier of New South Wales from 1877 to 1878.

There are two delightful ironies in the story of James Squire.

The first is that he was one of only a few ex-convicts to be ever appointed a constable. After half a lifetime of thieving and stealing as a way of life, he applied to be made a constable for the district of Eastern Farms on the grounds that there was too much stealing and thieving going on in the area, especially from his properties!

When he managed to cultivate a hop vine in 1806, from plants he had been given a few years before, he took the first small crop to Governor King. The governor's joy was unbounded at this sign of hope that the rum trade might one day be a thing of the past in New South Wales.

Governor King was so delighted at Squire's achievement, in fact, that he gave a directive which any gypsy, transported for stealing nine chooks, would have appreciated . . . in more ways than one.

The governor directed that a 'cow be given to Mr Squire from the Government herd'.

# SWEENEY

## Henry Lawson

It was somewhere in September, and the sun was going down,
When I came, in search of 'copy', to a Darling-River town;
'Come-and-have-a-drink' we'll call it—'tis a fitting name,
    I think—
And 'twas raining, for a wonder, up at Come-and-have-a-
    drink.
'Neath the public-house verandah I was resting on a bunk
When a stranger rose before me, and he said that he was drunk;
He apologised for speaking; there was no offence, he swore;
But he somehow seemed to fancy that he'd seen my face
    before.
'No erfence,' he said. I told him that he needn't mention it,
For I might have met him somewhere; I had travelled round
    a bit,
And I knew a lot of fellows in the bush and in the streets—
But a fellow can't remember all the fellows that he meets.
Very old and thin and dirty were the garments that he wore,
Just a shirt and pair of trousers, and a boot, and nothing
    more;
He was wringing-wet, and really in a sad and sinful plight,
And his hat was in his left hand, and a bottle in his right.
His brow was broad and roomy, but its lines were somewhat
    harsh,

42

And a sensual mouth was hidden by a drooping, fair
    moustache;
(His hairy chest was open to what poets call the 'wined',
And I would have bet a thousand that his pants were gone
    behind).
He agreed: 'Yer can't remember all the chaps yer chance to
    meet,'
And he said his name was Sweeney—people lived in
    Sussex-street.
He was campin' in a stable, but he swore that he was right,
'Only for the blanky horses walkin' over him all night.'
He'd apparently been fighting, for his face was black-and-
    blue,
And he looked as though the horses had been treading on
    him, too;
But an honest, genial twinkle in the eye that wasn't hurt
Seemed to hint of something better, spite of drink and rags
    and dirt.
It appeared that he mistook me for a long-lost mate of his—
One of whom I was the image, both in figure and in phiz—
(He'd have had a letter from him if the chap were living still,
For they'd carried swags together from the Gulf to Broken
    Hill).
Sweeney yarned awhile and hinted that his folks were doing
    well,
And he told me that his father kept the Southern Cross
    Hotel;
And I wondered if his absence was regarded as a loss
When he left the elder Sweeney—landlord of the Southern
    Cross.
He was born in Parramatta, and he said, with humour grim,
That he'd like to see the city 'ere the liquor finished him,
But he couldn't raise the money. He was damned if he could
    think
What the Government was doing. Here he offered me a drink.
I declined—'*twas* self-denial—and I lectured him on booze,

Using all the hackneyed arguments that preachers mostly use;
Things I'd heard in temperance lectures (I was young and
	rather green),
And I ended by referring to the man he might have been.
Then a wise expression struggled with the bruises on his face,
Though his argument had scarcely any bearing on the case:
'What's the good o' keepin' sober? Fellers rise and fellers fall;
What I might have been and wasn't doesn't trouble me at all.'
But he couldn't stay to argue, for his beer was nearly gone.
He was glad, he said, to meet me, and he'd see me later on;
He guessed he'd have to go and get his bottle filled again,
And he gave a lurch and vanished in the darkness and the
	rain.
And of afternoons in cities, when the rain is on the land,
Visions come to me of Sweeney with his bottle in his hand,
With the stormy night behind him, and the pub verandah-
	post—
And I wonder why he haunts me more than any other ghost.
Still I see the shearers drinking at the township in the scrub,
And the Army praying nightly at the door of every pub,
And the girls who flirt and giggle with the bushmen from
	the West—
But the memory of Sweeney overshadows all the rest.
Well, perhaps it isn't funny; there were links between us
	two—
He had memories of cities, he had been a jackaroo;
And, perhaps, his face forewarned me of a face that I might
	see
From a bitter cup reflected in the wretched days to be.
I suppose he's tramping somewhere where the bushmen
	carry swags,
Cadging round the wretched stations with his empty
	tucker-bags:
And I fancy that of evenings, when the track is growing dim,
What he 'might have been and wasn't' comes along and
	troubles him.

# A LETTER TO *THE BULLETIN*

## Henry Lawson

'Australians are not a nation of snobs like
the English, or of extravagant boasters
like the Americans . . . they are simply a
nation of drunkards.'

Marcus Clarke, 1869

Dear *Bulletin*,

I'm awfully surprised to find myself sober. And, being sober, I take up my pen to write a few lines, hoping they will find you as well as I am at present. I want to know a few things. In the first place: Why does a man get drunk? There seems to be no excuse for it. I get drunk because I'm in trouble, and I get drunk because I've got out of it. I get drunk because I am sick, or have corns, or the toothache: and I get drunk because I'm feeling well and grand. I got drunk because I was rejected; and I got awfully drunk the night I was accepted. And, mind you, I don't like to get drunk at all, because I don't enjoy it much, and suffer hell afterwards. I'm always far better and happier when I'm sober, and tea tastes better than beer. But I get drunk. I get drunk when I feel that I want a drink, and I get drunk when I don't. I get drunk because I had a row last night and made a fool of myself and it worries me, and when things are fixed up I get drunk to celebrate it. And, mind you, I've got no craving for drink. I get drunk because I'm frightened about things, and because

45

I don't care a damn. Because I'm hard up and because I'm flush. And, somehow, I seem to have better luck when I'm drunk. I don't think the mystery of drunkenness will ever be explained—until all things are explained, and that will be never. A friend says that we don't drink to feel happier, but to feel less miserable. But I don't feel miserable when I'm straight. Perhaps I'm not perfectly sober just now, after all. I'll go and get a drink, and write again later.

# THE PROMISE

## E.G. Murphy ('Dryblower')

'Give me your word,' a wife implored
Of a scribe well-known round here;
'You'll never again invite my dad
To take the drink that sends him mad
And brings his ruin near.'
'I promise you,' solemnly said the scribe,
And a truthful scribe is he,
'Never again!' and he raised his lid,
'Will I ask him out to take a tid . . .
I'll wait till your dad asks me.'

# ANZAC NIGHT IN THE GARDENS

## Lennie Lower

> If on my theme I rightly think,
> There are five reasons we should drink:
> Good wine; a friend; because we're dry;
> Or lest we should be by and by;
> Or—any other reason why.
>
> Reverend Henry Aldrich, c.1695

Lost in the wilds of the Botanic Gardens! Heavens, shall we ever forget it! The last human face we saw was that of Matthew Flinders, the great explorer.

We got in with a few Anzacs last night, and we forget how we got into the Gardens, but believe us, it's terrible. Instructive, but terrible.

Nothing to drink but goldfish.

Bottle-trees dotted about the place, and we had no opener. Naked men and women standing on square whitewashed rocks. All dumb!

We wandered up to a signboard, thinking to read, 'Ten miles to . . .' and saw there, 'Please do not walk on the grass borders.'

Starving, practically, we climbed a coconut tree for food and found it was a date tree without any dates on it.

We came to a tree marked 'Dysoxylum'. We thought, we *knew*, how sox were dyed, but what shall it profit a man if he lose himself in the Gardens?

We came to where the tortoise slept, and knocked on his shell. Like all the rest of our friends, he was in, but he didn't answer.

Dawn found us clawing at the front of the Herbarium, shrieking hysterically for just a little thyme.

The keeper who found us said that everything was all right and this was the way out. We don't know what became of the others.

Probably their bodies will be found in the bandstand and identified by their pawn tickets. The Anzacs certainly were, and still are, a tough crowd. We will never go into the Gardens again without wearing all our medals and two identification discs.

It's always best to carry a spare on Anzac night.

# LIFESPAN

**Anonymous**

Horse and mule live thirty years
And nothing know of wines and beers.
Goats and sheep at twenty die,
Never tasting Scotch or rye.
The cow drinks water by the ton,
And at eighteen is mostly done.
The dog at sixteen cashes in
Without the aid of rum or gin.
The cat in milk and water soaks
And then, in twelve short years, it croaks.
The sober, modest, bone-dry hen
Lays eggs for nogs, then dies at ten.
The animals are strictly dry,
They sinless live and swiftly die.
While sinful, gin-full, rum-soaked men
Survive for three score years and ten.
And some of us, though mighty few,
Stay pickled till we're ninety-two.

# THE 99TH REGIMENT ARE REVOLTING

Jim Haynes

> 'Drink, sir, is a great provoker . . . It provokes
> the desire, but it takes away the performance.'
>
> Shakespeare, *Macbeth*, Act 2, Scene 3

There's been a lot of trouble over access to alcohol in Australia's history, notably the Rum Rebellion and the Valentine's Day soldiers' riot of 1916. So it's not surprising to learn that, in 1846, the first 'strike' in our history by an entire regiment was precipitated by the withdrawal of their grog ration.

The 99th Regiment of Foot was formed in the county of Lanarkshire, in the lowlands of Scotland, in 1825. At that time the county included the city of Glasgow, long famous for producing hard-drinking, pugnacious men.

Three detachments were sent to the colonies of New South Wales and Van Diemen's Land in 1842 aboard the convict ships *John Renwick*, *Candahar* and *North Briton*. The regiment served as 'convict guards' at Sydney, Parramatta, Hobart, Moreton Bay and Norfolk Island between 1843 and 1856 and fought in the Maori War in 1845.

In command of these tough Scots was an Englishman, Henry Despard, an overbearing martinet whose reputation in Australian colonial military history was established by two major errors of judgement.

Born in 1784 in Devon, Despard seems to have been the arche-typal upper-class twit! His military tactics were decades out of date and his attitude towards the lower classes, other races and lower ranks was mind-bogglingly snobbish and reactionary, even by the standards of his time.

Commissioned as an ensign in the 17th Regiment of Foot in 1799, Despard saw active service in several campaigns in India between 1808 and 1818, and became a brigade major in 1817. He rose to a lieutenant colonel in 1829, and was inspecting officer of the Bristol recruiting district for four years from 1838. In 1842 he took command of a detachment of the 99th Regiment of Foot, stationed in Sydney.

On 1 June 1845 Despard and two companies of his regiment arrived in Auckland in response to an appeal for assistance by Governor Robert FitzRoy after attacks by Maori led by rebel chief Hone Heke, who had grievances resulting from the implementa-tion of the Treaty of Waitangi. These attacks escalated into what was known as the Flagstaff War or Northern War.

Despard was given the temporary rank of colonel and took command of all British troops in New Zealand. On 8 June he sailed for the Bay of Islands with more than 600 men. They established a base at the Waimate mission station and began to bombard Ohaeawai, the first Maori pa designed to resist artillery fire. Its 100-strong garrison was protected by a complex of bunkers and trenches.

On 1 July the Maori made a daring attack, which prompted Despard to charge that afternoon, although no significant breach had been made in the stockade. He used the old-fashioned Napo-leonic War tactics, with his troops advancing shoulder to shoulder.

The British attack made no impression on the virtually undam-aged main stockade, and Despard was forced to order a recall. More than 120 of his men were killed or wounded in this action. Despard at first blamed his men's failure to carry axes and other tools as he had ordered, but he later conceded that his plan had had little chance of success.

Despard then attempted to negotiate a peaceful settlement but failed. Although he now had a force of around 1300 British troops, several hundred Maori warriors and substantial artillery support, the Northern War ended soon after without any British victories and Despard returned to New South Wales.

Despard's performance during the campaigns of 1845 was woeful. The British force is often described in the history of the war as 'ineptly led'. Despard was bad-tempered, impatient and obstinate and had a contempt for the Maori, which led him to underestimate his opponents. When Maori chief Waka Nene, one of the many chiefs who sided with the British, offered his services to help the campaign, Despard replied that when he 'required the assistance of savages', he would ask for it.

The position of commander of British troops during the Northern War had been given to a man of 60 who had not seen active service for nearly 30 years and was unequal to the task. Apart from his ineptitude, Despard suffered from neuralgia. His decision to attack Ohaeawai was one of the most incompetent and tragic in British military history—prompted more by a fit of temper than by any military considerations.

After his miserable performance in the Maori Wars, Colonel Henry Despard returned to Sydney, where his leadership failures continued and he was to provoke the infamous mutiny of the 99th Regiment in 1846.

The mutiny was a protest against Colonel Despard's decision to discontinue the daily allowance of grog normally supplied to troops on foreign service. It was, in fact, also a protest against his over-officious style of leadership and his attempts to separate the troops from the townspeople.

Evidently Despard was of the opinion that the troops might have to be used against the unruly ex-convict population, and therefore he did not want them to be seen as a part of the general community.

The locals, in Despard's opinion, were much too fond of alcohol. He thought that the 'foreign service' grog ration encouraged the troops to fraternise far too much with the people they were there to control. It is also probably true that he wasn't overly fond of the unruly men of the Lanarkshire regiment he commanded.

Despard also gave an order that prohibited citizens from walking on any part of the grass-covered area in front of the barracks when listening to the band play. Thursday afternoon performances of the barracks' band had been the town's chief entertainment for many years, but Despard thought it 'unmilitary' and likely to lead to dangerous fraternising.

The old military quarters in Sydney were known as the George's Square Barracks. They covered an area including Wynyard Square on the western side of George Street and eastern side of Clarence Street, from Barrack Street to Margaret Street. The entrance gate was on the western side of George Street at the junction of York and Barrack streets.

The 99th were so annoyed when the wowserish Despard stopped their grog ration that, according to General Sir Maurice O'Connell, they 'forgot their obligations to their Queen and country, by refusing to obey the lawful commands of their Officers, or to perform any further duty'.

When Despard reported the developments to O'Connell, who was overall commander of troops in the Australian colonies and lived in Sydney, the general went to the barracks and threatened to arm the convicts working on Cockatoo Island dockyards and march them against the mutineers.

But instead of backing down, the 99th took up their arms and took over the barracks, compelling the general and his officers to leave.

The general then forwarded a despatch to Colonel Bloomfield of the 11th Regiment in Hobart, directing him to proceed to Sydney without delay, with as many men as could be spared, to disarm the mutineers of the 99th Regiment.

The 11th Regiment of Foot was a battle-hardened regiment from Devonshire, in the south of England; they had fought in the Peninsular Wars and were known as the 'Bloody Eleventh'. Unlike the 99th, they were a popular regiment with the people of the colonies and would eventually replace the 99th in Sydney.

The barque *Tasmania* was chartered and 400 men and officers embarked for Sydney. Three days later they were in sight of Sydney

Heads but an offshore gale kept the vessel from entering the heads for seven days.

Meanwhile, the 99th Regiment somehow learned that a vessel full of troops was outside of Sydney Heads and, knowing the game was up, offered to return to duty.

The 11th Regiment arrived in Sydney on 8 January 1846, approximately four weeks since the mutiny began. They marched four deep, with fixed bayonets, along George Street, with the band playing 'Paddy Will You Now', till they halted at the barracks' main gate.

Expecting resistance from the mutineers, they entered Barrack Square to a most hearty welcome and cheers from the 99th Regiment and their women and children, together with as many citizens as could fit into the barrack grounds.

Thus ended the mutiny of the 99th Regiment.

The 11th Regiment then gave a sumptuous dinner to the citizens of Sydney, their wives and children, with entertainment consisting of old English sports, games and other amusements.

The grog ration was restored to the 99th Regiment, and Sydney's citizens were again allowed to walk on the grass in front of Barrack Square and listen to the band play on Thursday afternoons.

On 2 July 1846, Despard, like many other useless upper-class twits, was knighted for his 'services', and in 1854 he was promoted to major-general; he then retired from the army. He died at Heavitree in Devon, England, in 1859.

The 99th Regiment were transferred to Van Diemen's Land in 1848 and remained there until 1856 (the year the colony changed its name to Tasmania).

The first war memorial in Australia was erected in Hobart in 1850. It is dedicated to the 24 men of the 99th Regiment who were killed serving under Henry Despard in New Zealand in 1845.

The impressive monument still stands today. It was paid for by subscriptions from the men of the regiment, and the foundation stone was laid and piously dedicated at a solemn service on Monday, 27 May 1850 by none other than—you guessed it—Colonel Henry Despard who, according to the *Colonial Times* of Hobart:

. . . addressed the troops in allusion to the object before them, observing, that a good soldier who may fall in the service of His Sovereign and Country, will not be forgotten, but his memory will be held in grateful recollection, by his comrades who survive to share the laurels, he has assisted to purchase with his life.

To which he might have added . . . 'aided by my inept leadership'.

# YOU CAN'T TAKE IT WITH YOU

## Anonymous

There are many good reasons for drinking—
And one has just entered my head:
If a man doesn't drink when he's living,
How the hell can he drink when he's dead!

# MR SLOOVE'S SPEECH
# [FROM *HERE'S LUCK*]

## Lennie Lower

> 'Beware the evils of temperance and sobriety
> and embrace the worship of the bottle!'
>
> David Ireland, 1971

The party had quietened down considerably. There was a strip-poker party in the dining room and a drinking party in the bedroom adjoining. Couples whispered here and there in corners, a few stupid ones sang determinedly around the piano and the weaker vessels slept and mumbled in strange attitudes. I strolled past the strip-poker table, noticing as I passed that most of the girls evidently could not play poker . . .

I found myself a couple of bottles of whisky and sat down.

'You're not going to drink that on your own?' exclaimed Temple, who was lying on the floor next to me with his head propped up on his elbow.

'There's plenty over there for you,' I replied, pointing to the stack.

'But, man, you'll kill yourself!'

'I'm not worrying about that,' I said, putting the bottle to my mouth . . .

'Am I to sit here and watch a man drink himself to death!' shouted Temple. 'I say nothing against a man drinking, but to drink like that . . . Mr Sloove,' he said, pointing to the politician, 'and myself are the only two sober men here!'

'Gentlemen,' announced Mr Sloove. 'Mr Temple has just mentioned my name to you and accused me of being sober. I must admit the charge . . . Knowing that Mr Gudgeon is a gentleman well liked and respected in the locality, and an old resident of the district, I thought to seize the opportunity of combining business with pleasure by addressing a few remarks—'

. . . Mr Sloove seemed to have captured the interest of the assembly.

'Of course,' he was saying, 'there are people who will never drink. Subnormal freaks, or misguided in their early youth.

'There are others who may be converted,' continued Mr Sloove.

'I have to my eternal credit one outstanding case. He was a miserable man for whom life held but little interest. Taciturn and morose, he was, wrapped in his petty ideas of life and pleasure. In fact, gentlemen, he had never had a proper drink in his life.'

There was a mutter of amazement from the audience. I noticed the young man from the *Daily Herald* taking shorthand notes.

(Our party was described as an orgy and a saturnalia in the next evening's paper. The hound! I got a copy of Mr Sloove's speech from him, though. Best speech I ever heard.)

'I persuaded this man,' continued Sloove, 'to taste, just taste my fine old brandy, two cases of which comprised my late father's estate. He was run over by a bus and couldn't finish it. He died a broken-hearted man. Sometimes I think he haunts the cellar, spirit calling to spirit, but I digress.

'I offered this poor, water-logged waif the brandy.

'He smelt it. He sipped it. He sipped again, eagerly. He tossed it off. Then turning to me, he clasped my hand, a look of reverent wonder in his eyes. "To think . . ." he said, "all these years. And I never knew. I never knew! . . . *Fill it up again!*"'

A burst of cheers awoke Simpson, who started to clap.

'Now, any night, I can go to his flat and find him lying under the table, happy.'

The speaker waved his hand.

'Alcohol! The last gift of the relenting gods. The simple word that makes life's crossword puzzle easier to elucidate.'

'How many paltry figures have ranted against it, shrieked their censure,' he cried, 'and faded back to the earth from which they come—to fertilise the vines.

'Gaze on your glass of beer.'

We gazed.

'See how the lambent, lazy bubbles drift to the top, as men drift through life; linger a while in the froth, and burst of old age, or are cut off in their prime in Fate's thirsty gulp. This scourge, this shame, this liquid degradation, what is it?'

''Ere!' protested Simpson, angrily.

'It links the extremes of mankind in one common friendly girdle. The labourer disturbing the rocks of ages with his pick, and Shakespeare in his favourite inn, and Attila, the Scourge of God, who died of too much mead.'

'What's this mead? Where c'n it be got?'

'Look here, Simpson,' I whispered. 'Don't interrupt again. This man's a genius. Listen to him.'

'Noah,' shouted Sloove, 'the greatest navigator of all times; cooped in the ark with his relations and a lot of other wild animals, drifting in a landless world. Chosen from countless teetotallers drowned in their favourite drink; he landed at last on the lonely peak of Ararat. When the awful responsibility of beginning a new world had eased, what happened?

'The Bible says that his son found him lying in the vineyard, his back teeth awash and a happy, boozed smile on his face.

'Behold your Robbie Burns. He died. Certainly, who doesn't? He drank himself to death! What of it? For every man who dies of drink, a thousand die of dinner-distended stomachs. Ask the man who owns one.'

'What the hell are you looking at me for?' I demanded, as Stanley eyed my vest with a silly grin on his face.

'Says the earnest reformer,' continued Sloove, 'supposing that, instead of drinking whisky, you drank milk. Look at the benefits to your health, your pocket, and the race in general. Against this horrible suggestion there is, thank heaven, a stonewall fact, a gesture in granite, one great unshakeable answer, "I don't like milk."

'It is an axiom of economists that supply follows demand like the blood follows a punch on the nose. We want beer. Therefore there is beer. Peer into the murky mystery of your orange phosphate drink. What do you see? A chemical laboratory. A bit of this being added, a bit of that tipped in. And in the translucent depths of booze? Hop fields, rippling acres of barley, and whistling boys in the sunshine, picking grapes. You would have me drink this coloured eye lotion? Consider, then, this awful possibility.

'Two old friends meet.

'"Bill! Why, you old son of a gun!"

'"Where've you been? Haven't seen you for years!"

'A moment of happy grins, of surging happy memories, of handshakes truly meant.

'"Well, well, well!"

'Glad. Awkward. Lost for words.

'"Come and have an orangeade!"'

He paused, while a wave of horror swept over the company.

'I *ask* you!' he exclaimed passionately . . .

'Alcohol is a necessity,' he said. 'The craving for food is recognised as legitimate, even though the rabid vegetarian seeks to snatch the chop from his brother's mouth. Yet I am asked to satisfy my desire for a drink with water! Water! Empty jam tins are all right for goats, but a hungry dog wants meat. We are but dust, add water and we are mud.

'Why, when the world was first made it was all water, until the mistake was seen and rectified, and land made available for hop growing.'

'Of course,' agreed Simpson.

'I don't want to disparage water. It is an excellent medium for sailing boats in, washing, cooking and irrigation. It is an ingredient of most liquors. But to drink it in its raw state! Watch a drinking fountain in Pitt Street. You'll stand for hours and see it undisturbed, save for the mooning messenger boy who stamps on the button to see the water squirt.

'As to those who have tasted liquor and liked it not, well, they do exist; but about them we need not bother. They are akin to the horse that drinks water and the calf that guzzles milk. Evolution will weed them out. Lack of the booze taste is lack of virility and they cannot survive. Is there any more expressive word in our language than "Milksop"? And what is it but a weak sopper of milk, a lemonade lapper, a cocoa gargler?

'"Yo! Ho! And a bottle of raspberry!" Absurd, isn't it?'

'My oath, it is.'

'Despite our modern education there are fools who have never tasted drink, lunatics who have, and don't like it, and plague spots, positive menaces, who seek to abolish it!'

There was a general movement of uneasiness.

'Ah, friends. If you would learn, come with me beneath the bough. I'll bring the bread and the wine thou. I can't bear all the expense. We shall transform that wilderness and people it with pink lizards and blue monkeys with hats on. Be saved while the thirst is still on you and you shall have access to a land where every prospect pleases, and only closing time is vile.

'And I, when I have sunk my last pot, when my foot no more rests on the rail, and old Time calls, "Six o'clock, sir!", then carry me to the strains of the "Little Brown Jug" and lay me on my bier . . . "And in a winding-sheet of vine-leaf wrapt, so bury me by some sweet garden-side."

'Till then . . . Here's luck!'

There was a moment's silence, then suddenly the assembly burst into a roar of delighted applause. They stamped their feet, whistled piercingly, and cheered and clapped.

Mr Sloove smiled, and attempting a bow, fell off the chair. There were a dozen hands to help him rise.

# THE CONVICTS' RUM SONG

## Anonymous

Cut yer name across me backbone,[1]
Stretch me skin across a drum,
Iron me up on Pinchgut Island[2]
From today till Kingdom Come!
I will eat yer Norfolk dumpling[3]
Like a juicy Spanish plum,
Even dance the Newgate Hornpipe[4]
If ye'll only gimme RUM!

---

1   Convicts were often flogged until the bone showed.
2   Convicts hanged on Pinchgut Island (originally Rock Island, later levelled to build Fort Denison) were left to hang in 'gibbets' (chains) until the skeletons fell apart—this practice was abolished in 1835.
3   Tasteless cornmeal porridge served before dawn to convicts.
4   The 'death dance' of men being hanged—their legs kicked as they strangled on the gallows.

# SECTION TWO
## UNDER THE INFLUENCE

# WHEN IS A MAN DRUNK?

## Anonymous

He is not drunk who, from the floor,
Can rise and drink and ask for more;
But drunk is he who speechless lies,
Without the strength to drink or rise.

# SNAKES AND ALCOHOL

## Kenneth Cook

> 'I always keep a supply of stimulant handy in
> case I see a snake—which I also keep handy.'
>
> W.C. Fields, 1930

'There's two things that don't mix,' said Blackie slowly and pompously, 'snakes and alcohol.'

It would never have occurred to me to mix them but I nodded solemnly. Nod solemnly is pretty well all you can do when you're talking to a snake man because they never actually converse— they just tell you things about snakes.

Blackie was a travelling snake man. He travelled in a huge pantechnicon which had wooden covers on the sides. Whenever he found a paying audience—a school or a tourist centre—he would drop the wooden covers and reveal a glass-walled box the size of a large room. This was his snake house, inhabited by a hundred or so snakes ranging from the deadly taipans and browns to the harmless tree snakes.

Blackie was like all the snake men I've ever met, cadaverously thin, very dirty, extremely shabby and without a second name. I think he was called Blackie because of his fondness for black snakes, or perhaps because his eyes were jet black—he had the only eyes I've seen that were black. He looked as though his enormous pupils had supplanted his irises, but if you looked closely you could see the faint outline of the black pupils inside them. I tended to feel uncomfortable looking into those two round patches of black and the suffused and bloodshot eyes (all snake men have suffused and bloodshot eyes—I think it's because snakes bite them so often).

I met Blackie just north of Mackay in Queensland where we were both camping on a little-known beach named Macka's Mistake; I don't know why it's named that. I was trying to finish a novel and Blackie was doing something complicated with the air conditioning of his pantechnicon, so we were thrown together for about a fortnight and became firm friends.

Blackie was so good and confident with snakes that he imbued me with much of his own attitude. I would often go into his snake house, sit on a log and talk to him while lethal reptiles regarded us torpidly within striking distance or slid gracefully and slowly away from the smell of our tobacco smoke.

Now and then a black, brown or green snake would slide softly past my foot and Blackie would say, 'Just sit there and don't move. It won't bite you if you don't move.' I wouldn't move and the snake wouldn't bite me. So, after a time, I became more or less relaxed with the snakes, provided Blackie was there.

Nothing would have induced me to go into the snake cage without Blackie, but I was convinced he could actually talk to the things, or at any rate communicate with them in some way which both he and they understood. It seemed to me at times fancifully possible that Blackie might have some drops of snake blood in his veins. Or perhaps the venom he had absorbed made him somehow *simpatico* with the creatures. Mind you, I did notice that the snakes had black eyes too, and that made me wonder.

There was only one other camper at Macka's beach, Alan Roberts, a fat and friendly little photographer who had set up a tent and was making a study of seabirds. He, Blackie and I would usually meet in my campervan for drinks in the evening.

Only the previous night, Blackie had been expounding to me and Alan the dangers of mixing alcohol and snakes. Of course, this took place over a bottle of whisky and I was considerably disconcerted when I called on him in the morning to find him unconscious in his own snake house, two empty whisky bottles by his side and his body festooned with deadly snakes.

The snakes were lying quite still, apparently enjoying the warmth of Blackie's motionless body. I assumed he was alive because of the snores that shook the glass windows of the snake house. But I had no idea whether he had been bitten and was in a coma, or had simply drunk himself insensible, or both.

The snakes resting on Blackie were, as far as I could make out: one taipan (absolutely deadly) two king browns (almost as deadly) a death adder (very deadly) three black snakes (deadly) and one diamond snake (harmless).

My first impulse was to run screaming for help, but there was nobody in sight, and if Blackie jerked or turned in his drunken or moribund torpor, at least seven deadly snakes would probably sink their fangs into him simultaneously. Then, no doubt, the other eighty or ninety variably venomous snakes would stop lying peacefully round the snake house and join the fray. Blackie's chances of survival would be slight.

I knew the snake-house door did not lock. Normally when not in use it was covered by a wooden shutter, so I knew I could get in. But did I want to?

I didn't consider that in his present state Blackie would be able to provide his normal protection against snakes. Going in with Blackie like this would be worse than going in alone. A treacherous voice within me whispered that it would be better to run away and let Blackie wake up naturally. The snakes were used to him and he would probably instinctively act in the proper way with them.

Sadly, the treacherous voice wasn't convincing. Besides, I didn't know whether Blackie had already been bitten and needed medical help urgently.

I looked around for a weapon. Under the pantechnicon I saw a rake that Blackie used for clearing his snake house. I picked it up and cautiously and very slowly opened the door. There were several snakes between me and Blackie and I wasn't sure of their species. They all looked lethal. I poked at them gently with the rake and all of them, except one, resentfully slithered off to the other side of the snake house with no apparent intention except of going back to sleep. The one, a big king brown, raised itself on its coils and began hissing, throwing its head back to strike. I knew enough about snakes now to know that as long as I stayed the length of the snake's body away from its fangs, they couldn't reach me. Equally I knew that if I tried to pass this snake to get at Blackie, it could get to me.

I poked at it with the rake again and it struck, its fangs making a tiny ringing sound against the iron prongs. Blackie had told me that this sort of thing was bad for a snake's fangs. I didn't care. I poked at it again and it sank to the ground, wriggled over to Blackie, worked its way onto his back, then coiled again and began looking at me threateningly. It seemed much more agitated than before; no doubt its teeth hurt. The snakes already using Blackie as a mattress stirred fitfully, but didn't go anywhere.

A black snake detached itself from a group near the wall and came towards me. I banged it with the rake and it retired, probably mortally hurt. Again, I didn't care.

The king brown was hissing like a leaking steam pipe and the death adder appeared to dislike this. It made its way off, taking a path over Blackie's motionless head. There were still eight snakes on Blackie, seven of which were deadly.

I pushed tentatively at the king brown and it reared back, but didn't strike again. The movement disturbed the diamond snake and it went off to a quieter place. But that wasn't any real advantage, as it was harmless anyway.

A couple more black snakes started circling the walls and I remembered that the door behind me was open. There was a reasonable chance that within minutes the population of the snake house would be ravening around Macka's Mistake beach. I preferred they should escape rather than remain in the snake house with me, but I didn't want them waiting just outside when, if ever, I managed to drag Blackie through the door. I banged the rake on the floor in front of them. They stopped, considered this phenomenon, then retreated. I went back and pushed the door almost to.

What was Blackie's great maxim about snakes? Handle them very gently and slowly and they'll never bite you. I eyed the waving, hissing, tongue-flicking king brown on Blackie's back and decided I didn't believe this. Possibly if this king brown would just vacate Blackie's back I might be able to prod the rest away, gently and slowly.

However, the king brown showed no inclination to move and it was so angry now I felt that if Blackie so much as twitched an ear it would have him. I was sweating with terror and the rake handle was slippery in my grasp. The tension in my body was so great I knew that if I didn't solve this quickly I would collapse or run weeping from the snake house.

The devil with treating snakes slowly and gently, I thought; you can also treat them quickly and violently. I swung the rake at the weaving king brown with every intention of decapitating it if possible. It ducked. The rake missed. The snake struck. It became entangled with the prongs and I was holding the rake in the air with the king brown on the end of it. It sorted itself out quickly, coiled itself around the handle of the rake and began moving towards my hands. Convulsively I flung the rake away. It fell flat on Blackie's body, stirring the current inhabitants into a frenzy.

Fortunately, they all seemed to think they were being attacked by other snakes. They whipped up onto their coils and began threatening each other. Then, presumably trying for more advantageous positions, they all slipped off Blackie and began retreating towards the walls. Only one, the taipan, came near me.

All I could do was try the standard procedure of not moving and hope it would not notice that I was trembling uncontrollably. It went past and took up a position near the door.

Blackie was clear of snakes for the moment. He still hadn't moved. But now seemed safe to try to wake him.

'Blackie!' I screamed and prodded him with my foot. He didn't stir. 'Blackie!' I screamed again and kicked him hard in the ribs. He still didn't stir.

All the snakes were awake and active now, but inclined to stay near the walls. The only immediate problem was the taipan against the almost-closed door. Obviously there was no chance of rousing Blackie, so I leaned down and grabbed him by the shoulders. He half turned and belched. The alcohol-loaded gust of breath was the only thing I have ever encountered to approach a camel's breath for sheer noxiousness. The rake was still across Blackie's back. I grabbed it with one hand and grabbed him by the collar with the other.

The collar came away in my hand. I grabbed him by his sparse hair, but there wasn't enough of it to get a good hold. I grabbed him by the back of his shirt. A great patch of it came away, revealing a bony, dirty yellow back. There was not much left to grab him by, so I took him by the hand and began hauling. Fortunately the hand held together.

Blackie was no great weight and I began inching him across the floor, brandishing the rake at the taipan guarding the door and desperately aware of the sea of serpents to my right and left and behind me.

A carpet snake, quite harmless, wriggled within a handspan of my right foot and I hit it with the rake out of sheer spite. I was close to the door, just out of range of the taipan, which showed no sign of moving. I pushed at it with the rake but it ducked disdainfully and stayed where it was, weaving slowly and keeping its evil eyes fixed, I was sure, on my bare, exposed and palpitating throat.

I was desperately tempted to throw Blackie at the taipan and probably would have done, except that it's hard to throw a man anywhere when you've only got him by the hand.

I had, of course, been bellowing my head off for help for some minutes now and it came in the form of Alan Roberts, the photographer who, seeing through the plate glass what was happening, gallantly flung open the door to come to my help.

The violently pushed door caught the taipan fair in the back of the neck and squashed it against the wall. I went through the door, hauling Blackie after me.

'What the bloody hell . . . ?' Alan was saying.

Blackie had somehow stuck on the steps of the snake house. The taipan, apparently undamaged by the door, was very close to his exposed ankle, which it was inspecting curiously. The other snakes were mercifully milling some distance away, hissing among themselves.

'Help me get him out!' I gasped. Alan went through my routine of trying to grab Blackie by the collar, hair and back of shirt and ended up with handfuls of collar, hair and shirt before he grabbed Blackie's other hand. Together we hauled him through the door and slammed it in the face of the taipan, which seemed anxious to follow.

Blackie folded into a grubby heap on the ground and I leaned against the glass and tried to start breathing, which I had apparently stopped doing some time before.

'Has he been bitten?' said Alan.

'I don't know,' I croaked. 'Get an ambulance.'

Alan, a competent man who was not about to ask foolish questions, turned to go. Blackie jackknifed to his feet, opened the door of the snake house and tried to go back in.

Alan and I grabbed him by the shoulders and slammed the door.

'Blackie!' shouted Alan. 'What's wrong with you?'

Blackie, immobilised, stared at the closed door bemusedly.

'He's very drunk,' I said. 'I don't know whether he's been bitten or not.' I was beginning to doubt it. I didn't think people came out of snake-poison comas quite so abruptly. If he was out of a coma.

'Blackie,' I said, 'are you awake? Has a snake bitten you?'

Blackie focused on me and said disdainfully, 'Snakes don't bite me.'

'I think he's just drunk,' I said quietly to Alan, and then to Blackie, 'Better come up to my campervan and lie down for a while, Blackie.'

'Sure,' said Blackie, 'just lie down in here.' And he turned and tried to get in with the snakes again. Alan and I grabbed him.

'Come on, Blackie, come up to the van and have a sleep.'

But Blackie had looked through the plate glass and seen his beloved snakes rushing backwards and forwards or coiled and waving and hissing.

'Something's wrong with my snakes!' he roared, and began to struggle with us to get free.

'Blackie, Blackie,' said Alan, 'take it easy. You've had a few drinks . . .'

''Course I've had a few drinks,' said Blackie. 'Can't a man have a few drinks?'

'Of course you can, Blackie,' I said soothingly, 'but you were passed out with snakes all over you. We just hauled you out.'

Blackie looked at me closely. 'So that's why my snakes are all upset,' he said.

'That's right, Blackie.'

Blackie thought about that. 'Ah well,' he said after a while, 'I suppose you meant no harm. Don't do it again, though.'

And the wretched man pulled away and tried to get in the door again. Alan and I could hold him easily, but we weren't prepared to do it indefinitely.

'Now listen, Blackie,' I said firmly, 'just come over to my van and have a few hours' sleep and you can come back to your snakes.'

'I'm going back to my snakes now,' said Blackie. 'Get your hands off me.'

We let him go, but Alan slipped between him and the door. Blackie considered this new problem.

'I'm going in there,' he said quietly and threateningly.

'Calm down, Blackie,' said Alan reasonably.

Blackie took a wild and ineffectual swipe at him. Alan and I looked at each other helplessly. I mouthed the word 'Police?' behind Blackie's back and Alan nodded regretfully.

'Can you keep him out of there?' I asked.

'Yes,' said Alan confidently. I thought he could, too; Blackie was far too drunk to put up much of a fight.

The trouble was I didn't know where the nearest telephone was. As far as I knew I might have to go into Mackay, eighty kilometres away.

I drove at incredible speed down to the highway and was delighted to see a police patrol car go past at the junction of the roads. I sped after it with my hand on the horn and it stopped.

I leaped out of my van and ran to the police car. Two solemn Queensland policemen, both fat, red-faced, without humour, eternally middle-aged, looked at me expressionlessly.

'I wonder, would you follow me?' I said breathlessly. 'I've got a friend who's very drunk and who wants to sleep with his snakes.'

There was a long pause.

'What?' said the two policemen eventually, simultaneously.

'I've got a friend who's very drunk who wants to sleep with his snakes,' I said again, but this time I could hear my own words.

There was another long pause.

'Could you explain a bit more, sir?' said the driver policeman. Even then I could wonder at the talent of policemen for using the word 'sir' as an insult.

'Oh the hell with it, it's too difficult to explain. Just follow me, will you? It's urgent.'

I thought they probably would follow me, if not necessarily for the reason I wanted them to. I was right. They did and we arrived back at Macka's Mistake to find Blackie pinned to the ground with Alan Roberts kneeling on his shoulders. The snake house was still a whirl of activity. Blackie was shouting obscenities with considerable eloquence. I don't say the policemen put their hands on their guns, but they looked as though they might any minute. It was all too difficult to explain, so I just gestured at the strange tableau of Blackie and Alan in front of the snake house.

'What seems to be the problem?' said one of the policemen.

Blackie stopped shouting when he saw the uniforms. Alan let him go and he stood up, stared for a moment then looked reproachfully and unbelievingly at me. 'You called the cops,' he accused.

'What is all this?' said the policeman.

Blackie saved the necessity for an explanation by feebly trying to punch the policeman's nose. They took him off to Mackay and charged him with being drunk and disorderly.

Alan and I waited through the day until we felt he must be reasonably sober and then went down and bailed him out. Blackie was silent until halfway through the journey back when he suddenly and tearfully asked, 'How could you do this to me?'

Alan and I explained the sequence of events to him. 'Is that true?' he said.

'Perfectly true, Blackie. We had to do it.'

'I can see that. Funny, I don't remember any of it.'

I tactfully made no reference to the two empty bottles of whisky.

'I'm really sorry,' Blackie said. 'Just goes to show, though, snakes and alcohol don't mix.'

# DRUNKS

## 'Syd Swagman'

Wild drunks, mild drunks, weary drunks and sad,
Drunks that 'knowed your dad, me son, when he was a lad,'
Tall drunks, small drunks, tubby drunks and thin.
Drunks that seem to cheek the cops until they get run in;
Square drunks, lair drunks, moody drunks and loud,
Drunks that will not drink with drunks because they are
     too proud.
Tough drunks, rough drunks, dirty drunks and fat,
Drunks that shicker with the flies and shicker on their pat;*
Poor drunks, sore drunks—heads as big as tanks,
Drunks that keep the town alive with their funny pranks;
Glad drunks, mad drunks, yellow drunks and white—
Somehow I meet a lot of drunks whenever I get tight.

* *The term 'shicker' is slang for drinking (it's Yiddish); 'with the flies' and 'on their pat' both mean 'alone'—i.e. 'with only the flies for company', and an abbreviation of 'Pat Malone' which is rhyming slang for 'alone'.*

# THE VALENTINE'S DAY MUTINY

## Jim Haynes

Few Australians today know that during World War I, 15,000 Australian recruits mutinied, defied orders, marched into Liverpool, took over the town and wrecked the hotels. Thousands then took the trains into Sydney and terrorised the city until ten o'clock at night. The New South Wales premier called an emergency cabinet meeting and the police rushed in 500 reinforcements from the suburbs. The army mobilised 1500 regular soldiers at Victoria Barracks and the showground, and a confrontation occurred at Central Railway Station in which seven men were shot and one was killed.

The date was February 14, 1916.

This event never gets a mention in any list of important events in our nation's history, yet the results were far-reaching. Hundreds of soldiers were sent to prison, 37 men were found guilty of various offences in civil courts, 280 were court-martialled and dismissed from the Australian Imperial Force (AIF) and the whole system of housing and training army recruits was overhauled.

Even more significant were the widespread and long-term social effects which resulted from this drunken mutiny. Four months after the day of the riot, the citizens of New South Wales overwhelmingly voted to close all pubs at 6 p.m.

---

In February 1916 the war was in its second year and the 'Little Digger', Prime Minister Billy Hughes, was calling for conscription and urging men to join up—and they were! Australia's population was 5 million in 1916 and 39 per cent of males aged 18 to 40 enlisted voluntarily in World War I—a staggering 420,000.

There were several reasons why so many Australian men responded so eagerly to the call to join up and fight a war in Europe.

One was the weather.

There had been a severe drought across Australia for seven years and many men living in rural areas had little to do. Grazing properties were largely unstocked, there were fewer crops to harvest and work was scarce in the bush. The prolonged drought was caused by El Niño events in 1911, 1913 and 1914, and continued until well into 1916 when it finally ended in some parts of the continent. But it wasn't officially over until heavy rains and flooding occurred across southeastern Australia in December 1916. By then, tens of thousands of men had already left the bush.

Other reasons for the large volunteer enlistment were cultural.

Cadet training in schools had been compulsory from 1910 for Australian boys after they turned twelve. This meant that nearly all Aussie boys had been trained in rudimentary military procedure, had shot a rifle, camped in tents and worn army uniform. So army life was not a mystery to them and many enjoyed playing soldiers. The teachers in charge of cadets had been trained by the army and most encouraged the boys to join up when war was declared.

Australia was 'more British than Britain' back then. Jingoism and a rather naive, sycophantic attitude to 'king and country' (and 'Empire') were promoted by the Anglican Church and the establishment generally. Most Australians believed Britain had every right to rule the Empire and could do no wrong. Men joined up to unthinkingly defend what they perceived to be 'right' against 'wrong'.

Then again, many men openly admitted they joined up to 'see the world' and others, as Banjo Paterson put it, 'for the sake of a fight'.

Whatever the reason, when Britain called, 420,000 Australians answered.

The response was almost too much. Training facilities were stretched to breaking point and new camps were established hastily throughout 1915 and 1916. Recruitment procedure, training, logistics and organisation were often slapdash and shoddy.

It seems that the Australian Army, only fifteen years on from being a separate group of colonial militia, had no idea how to organise and train large numbers of recruits for a proper war. The recruits were treated more like cadets or colonial militiamen than professional soldiers about to serve in a very serious international war—and that brings us to the mutiny of Valentine's Day 1916.

There were training facilities in Sydney at Randwick and Kensington racetracks and the showground, and a regular army facility at Victoria Barracks. But the main training camp for the Commonwealth forces was at Liverpool, on the western edge of Sydney. Established in 1903, it became inadequate due to heavy enlistment once war was declared. A new camp was set up in 1914, just a mile away at Casula, to train men for the Light Horse.

These camps drew a lot of young men to the area to enlist. Many were country boys and just eighteen years of age. Many others lied about their age. The youngest known member of the 1st AIF was James Martin, from Tocumwal on the Murray River, who enlisted at 14 years and 3 months, claiming he was 18. He died of typhoid at Gallipoli aged 14 years and 9 months. We know of more than twenty Australians who died in WWI before they were eighteen years of age. We will never know how many minors actually joined and served.

By February 1916 the war had been going on for more than eighteen months, yet conditions in the camps were still makeshift and facilities were stretched to the point where living conditions were barely tolerable. Infrastructure in the camps had not been extended and enlarged quickly enough to cope with the intake of recruits.

Many men in the camp at Casula thought they and their fellow recruits were getting a raw deal and deserved better conditions. They had joined up to fight and possibly die for their country, but most didn't even have mattresses to sleep on. They wanted better basic facilities and flexible leave, and they complained about excessive discipline and overwork. On top of all that, there was no 'wet' canteen at Casula, which meant the men, who were drilling and training 36 hours a week, could not have a beer unless they had leave to visit Liverpool.

To make matters worse, the recruits were aware that conditions at the nearby internment camp for enemy aliens at Holsworthy were better than those they had to endure at Liverpool and Casula training camps. Anti-German sentiment was running high and jingoism and discontent were easily aroused among the recruits when exaggerated rumours of the better conditions at Holsworthy were spread around the camps.

Thus the scene was set for mutiny.

The tipping point came when it was decided, at the highest military level, that more drilling and route marching were required to prepare the recruits for the Western Front. A new training syllabus was prepared, to be implemented at all AIF training camps on 14 February 1916.

When the men at Casula were told, on morning parade that day, that they would be required to train 40.5 hours in future, resentment spilled over into action.

The men rioted.

Well, the rioting actually came a little later. And what occurred was also variously called a 'strike', 'protest', 'march', 'demonstration', 'rally', 'mutiny' and 'riot'—take your pick.

What first transpired after the morning parade was a call to join a protest march, along the lines of a 'union strike', by a group of ringleaders. There are conflicting accounts about who these ringleaders were, and just how the organisation and process of arranging the mutiny was achieved. Evidently a deputation or representatives of the recruits delivered an ultimatum to Camp Commandant, Colonel Miller.

According to the *Sydney Morning Herald*, Colonel Miller 'told the men frankly that their grievances would be inquired into, and that during the inquiry the old syllabus would be reverted to'.

Apparently this was not enough for the disgruntled troops.

In its extensive coverage the next day, the *Sydney Morning Herald* reported:

> At breakfast-time yesterday about 5000 troops of the Australian Imperial Forces, camped at Casula, near Liverpool, refused duty and demanded the retraction of a new training syllabus which had been issued that morning. When it was explained to them that the new syllabus was a camp order issued from headquarters, and could not be treated in that cavalier fashion, almost the whole body of men marched out of the camp and on to the town of Liverpool.
>
> Arriving at Liverpool, the principal training camp of the Commonwealth, the men called to their colleagues there, and in a few minutes' time about 15,000 soldiers were on strike.

The number of 'protesters' that marched from Casula varies: while the *SMH* cited 5000, it was estimated to be as many as 7000 by the police and as few as 2500 by officers at the camp. Whatever their original number, after they marched into the Liverpool camp and urged the recruits there to join them, the mob became a massive 15,000 and, not surprisingly, it wasn't long before the rioting began.

———

We need to pause the narrative there for now, however, as there is some important backstory to be examined.

Liverpool Council, and the New South Wales Police Department, had been warning the army for almost a year that something like the Valentine's Day Riot was inevitable—and this wasn't the first time that men from the Liverpool and Casula camps had rioted.

As early as July 1915, the municipal council had asked for more police officers to be stationed at Liverpool, as about 6000 men were being trained in the district. In September a Sergeant Coates, stationed at Liverpool, reported that there were discipline problems at the military camps and pointed out that numbers at the camps had increased to 17,000 men. On Sundays an extra 15,000 visiting family members were also in Liverpool.

By the end of the year, the situation was set to explode. On Friday, 26 November there was a skirmish between sentries and men attempting to leave the camp at Casula, without leave passes, to have a drink in Liverpool.

Then, the following evening, about 400 soldiers on leave from camps caused a riot in the streets of central Sydney. Leading a crowd estimated at 1500, they attacked and damaged 'German' clubs and businesses in the CBD in ugly scenes of civil disorder.

The soldiers had assembled around 8 p.m. outside the Deutsche Club in Phillip Street, and twelve windows were smashed. The police dispersed the crowd but not long afterwards the soldiers marched down George Street and stopped at the Frankfurt Sausage Company shop, where one soldier kicked in the window and goods were stolen. (Hilariously, the Frankfurt Sausage Company was actually a retail outlet of a British-owned smallgoods firm that had a contract to supply the Department of Defence with foodstuff.)

Police apprehended the window smasher but the crowd intervened and he got away. As the mob moved towards Circular Quay, police arrested three soldiers, and not long after another fifteen soldiers and two civilians were arrested when the crowd moved up Elizabeth Street and started throwing stones at the Concordia Club.

The huge mob then followed the police and the arrested men to Central Police Station, where they demanded the release of the prisoners and threatened to attack the station. Police responded with a baton charge into the crowd, which dispersed. Some of the men proceeded to the building in Bathurst Street that housed the Socialist Club, and several of its windows were smashed. Two police were injured in the disturbances.

But there was more to come. On the following Monday, 29 November—five months after an official request from Liverpool Council for more police—their worst fears were realised when 1000 soldiers took over several pubs and caroused drunkenly in the streets of Liverpool.

When Police Inspector Musgrave and thirteen police officers arrived from Parramatta at 9.30 p.m. to deal with the problem, they found groups of men roaming the streets, laughing and singing and drinking from bottles stolen from several pubs. The scene at the Commercial Hotel was chaotic with drunken soldiers doing as they pleased, taking whatever they liked and passing the pub's supply of liquor to others in the street. At the Railway Hotel windows were smashed, and the Golden Fleece Hotel had been invaded and casks of beer stolen and taken into the street to be opened and their contents shared around. Also smashed were the windows of a shop owned by a Greek family and the windows of the last train leaving Liverpool for Sydney that evening.

Inspector Musgrave wisely avoided a direct standoff between his small band of police and the 1000 drunken soldiers and called the military to come and control their recruits. It took army officers one and a half hours to convince the soldiers to return to camp.

James Mitchell, Inspector General of Police, wrote a report to the Chief Secretary and the Premier's Department next day, headed 'Riotous conduct of soldiers at Liverpool on the 29th November 1915'. It stated that:

> The police repeatedly tried to reason with the men but they appeared to be completely out of control and paid no attention to advice. It was quite evident to the Inspector that had the Police made arrests serious trouble, and in all probability loss of life, would have ensued.

Mitchell warned New South Wales state administrators at the highest level that:

> As the resources of the Police Department are wholly inadequate to contend with hundreds of military men, many of them armed, I would strongly urge that the matter be at once brought officially under the notice of the military authorities.

He concluded the report by suggesting that the state government contact the army and officially:

... request that immediate steps be taken both to prevent destruction
of the property of law abiding citizens and to ensure law and order
being maintained by military men in our public thoroughfares.

Mitchell's prophetic warnings about civil disorder and loss of life
were ignored.

When a royal commission was finally established, it investi-
gated the complaints about the camp conditions at Liverpool
and Casula and made recommendations in a report. State Army
Commandant, Colonel Ramaciotti, inspected the camps and
promised better conditions and proper barracks instead of tents.
He also promised to heed the soldiers' complaints about the difficulty of obtaining leave and the availability of rail tickets.

The report, released in December 1915, noted that 53 soldiers
had died at the camp in the first nine months of that year; 48 from
measles, meningitis and pneumonia, and the other 5 from accidents and violence. One former commandant had refused to let
1500 men use straw to fill their mattress covers because he said it
made the camp 'untidy'. The commandant at the German Concen-
tration Camp at nearby Holsworthy agreed that his prisoners were
better clothed, housed and fed than regular army recruits.

As a result of the report, the federal defence department
decided to decentralise Liverpool and Casula camps.

Promises and plans were made, but little was done at the camps
in the short term. Meanwhile, there was more riotous and anti-
social behaviour involving army recruits in the city over the New
Year weekend. Then, just as James Mitchell had warned it might,
law and order broke down in Liverpool—and spread into the
heart of downtown Sydney.

———

The Valentine's Day Riot might have begun as some form of
'protest' or 'strike' but it soon developed along the same lines as
the 'riotous' behaviour of 29 November, except that the drinking
and pillaging began around 11 a.m. There was a whole day for the
rioting to spread and grow. Also, there were many more soldiers

involved this time, somewhere in the vicinity of 15,000, although levels of involvement and types of behaviour varied.

The thousands who marched into Liverpool eventually separated themselves into several groups. A large number stayed in Liverpool and ransacked the local pubs in a far more serious and violent way than had occurred in the previous riot. Their spree lasted about six hours and once again poor Inspector Musgrave did his best to reason with and restrain the men, with the help of a small band of about twenty police from Parramatta, Auburn and Lidcombe and an army chaplain. But Musgrave's men were ignored and, at one point, violently pushed aside by rioters. The *Sydney Morning Herald* gave this account next day:

**AT LIVERPOOL.**
**Damage at hotels.**
Trouble and disturbance that exceeded anything previously seen in Liverpool occurred yesterday. The men marched out of camp along Campbelltown road to Liverpool. A large body of men at once commenced to wreck the bar and adjoining parlours of the Commercial Hotel, and also the cellars, and succeeded in removing stock and inflicting damages which the licensee, Mrs. A. Isles, estimates at £2000. The men, after taking every available bottle of liquor in the bars, broke open the cellar, and hauled 11 hogsheads of beer, rum, wine, whisky, etc, out into Scott-street, where they were tapped, and pots and pans were taken from the hotel kitchen and used as drinking utensils.

A raid was also made on the bulk store where £1500 of stock was stored, and an axe was used to smash the doors and windows, but the efforts of the police blocked further robbery. Messrs. A. Comino and Co.'s premises were raided and the large plate glass windows smashed to atoms. The Golden Fleece Hotel was next made a mark for the men's attentions, and the licensee, Mr. J. J. Crowe, was left poorer by £700 worth of stock and damages by the now drink infuriated men.

Inspector Musgrave (Parramatta), with a small force of police, were powerless to interfere, but at 4 p.m. and in later trains from the city reinforcements of police under Inspector Barry arrived, and the men quietened down considerably.

Several attacks on the police were made; Constable Tillet, of Cabramatta, being punched about the face. Another soldier attempted to assault Constable Heckenberg, of Parramatta, but was promptly arrested.

During the morning the fruit and pie stalls in the street fronting Holsworthy bridge were wrecked, and the proprietors were forced to run for their lives, while bakers' and cordial carts were ransacked. At the railway station the men swarmed on to all the available trains armed with bottles and flasks, and all more or less in a state of intoxication; while in the streets of Liverpool men fought and struggled with one another. All the hotels were closed early in the morning, and police guards were stationed over them.

At the camp very little was doing, and some of the parades had to be abandoned. Tuesday is the usual pay-day for the men, and about £38,000 should be distributed, but in view of the conduct of the men it is doubtful whether this will be done.

The official police report indicates that the rioting in Liverpool continued unchecked from around 11 a.m. until 5 p.m. Inspector Musgrave reported:

On arrival I found the main streets thronged with men in military uniform, the majority of them more or less intoxicated. They had complete charge of the Commercial Hotel . . . intoxicated men were looting the liquor. The bar was wrecked and everything in it smashed and windows broken . . .

Previous to my arrival, Rafferty's Hotel had been looted . . .

Several attempts were then made to break into the Golden Fleece Hotel which the police were for a time able to prevent but being at last overwhelmed the rioters obtained an entrance and looted the contents.

The rioters next turned their attention to Penny's Hotel but by this time twenty additional police had arrived from Sydney, and with their assistance the attempt to break into this hotel was prevented, and also a raid on the Warwick Farm Hotel.

Some of the soldiers parading the streets climbed over the fence into a bakery and commenced throwing loaves of bread into the street to their comrades. The loaves were broken up and the crusts thrown at all and sundry, including Captain Smith who came up with another officer on horseback and tried to restrain the men . . .

About 5 pm, a considerable number of the soldiers having left for their camps, an opportunity arose for arresting four of the most aggressive of the rioters. Immediately an arrest was made the police were rushed and a struggle took place, bottles, blue metal were thrown, and several of the police had narrow escapes.

After a great deal of exertion the prisoners were lodged in the lockup. Shortly after Inspector Barry arrived from Sydney with twenty police. The arrival had the effect of preventing any further trouble, and the rioters gradually melted away.

Several thousand men 'melted away' from the action, either at Liverpool or later in Sydney, and eventually made their way back to camp. They abandoned the protest for several reasons. Some had second thoughts, others cold feet. Many who were coerced into joining, or joined in a spirit of mateship, were later unable to tolerate the behaviour of some of their fellow recruits or felt that their 'strike' had turned into a shambles and wished to disassociate themselves from the event. As the *Sydney Morning Herald* commented:

> It is perhaps only fair to point out that thousands of the men were absolutely dragooned into the meeting, and realised their position soon after reaching Sydney. Thousands of them retired quietly to their homes in the afternoon, and returned quietly to camp at night.

Leaving behind those whose only idea of a 'protest' was to ransack the local pubs in Liverpool and drink them dry, and those who were already melting away, the mass of recruits made for Liver-pool Railway Station and boarded the trains to Sydney. Most of the men who left the rioting at Liverpool to cause trouble in the city travelled between 1 p.m. and 4 p.m.

There were obviously some on board the trains who were motivated by the politics of the situation and genuinely wanted to protest about the conditions at the camps. It seems the plan was to march from Central Railway Station through the city to the Domain and conduct a 'rally' with speeches, and perhaps to take their concerns to Macquarie Street or some 'official' building.

Unfortunately their chances of achieving this goal were hindered by the fact that most of those who 'went along for the ride' were already quite inebriated and had little interest in the politics of the situation or the fairness or otherwise of what they were expected to do as army recruits. According to the *Sydney Morning Herald*:

> Among the train-load of soldiers were some of the rowdy type, and as usual on occasions of lawlessness, these asserted themselves on the journey down. Windows were smashed, and, notwithstanding the presence of women and children on the train, some of the men behaved like hoodlums.

A local witness in Liverpool, Mr Jones, of Junction Street, stated in a letter to police that the Commercial Hotel doors were forced open around 11.30 a.m. and later 'soldiers became demoniacs and by the 1.18 p.m. and 4 p.m. (trains) entrained for Sydney carrying flasks of spirits and beer with them which they had looted from this hotel'.

The *Sydney Morning Herald* described the scene as the rioters reached their destination:

> Arrived at Sydney, the soldiers formed up in a rough column of fours, and, headed by some men carrying flags, set off for the city, to the accompaniment of the discordant noise of trumpets and scraps of songs. Each succeeding train, as it arrived at Sydney,

was crammed with soldiers, many semi-drunk, and nearly all very noisy. One man nonchalantly sauntering along with two liquor measures, one under each arm, was arrested by some of the policemen on duty at the station and taken to No 2 Police Station, where he was charged.

It seems the 'official march' formed up before 2.30 p.m. and marched around the block via George Street, Hay Street and Elizabeth Street and back to Central Railway Station where others joined in.

Photos taken on the day show at least two groups marching behind flags. One group has several Union Jacks, battalion colours and a sign that reads 'Strike—We won't drill 40½ hours'. Another group was photographed marching behind a Union Jack flying from a sapling clothes prop, with a small triangular flag above.

Reading the *Sydney Morning Herald*'s version of events, it is easy to see how discipline broke down quite early and those attempting to 'organise' the chaos into a true protest march had an impossible task:

The last train from Liverpool prior to the cancellation of the service to the camp town was packed with soldiers. These, evidently under someone's leadership, quickly formed up in fours on the assembly platform. At the head of the long line were two buglers and two 'standard-bearers', one of the latter carrying the green and purple colours of the 5th Reinforcements of the 2nd Battalion, and the other holding aloft on a clothes prop the Union Jack, surmounted by a small red flag . . .

In a very short time the men had marched off the station down Pitt-street and into Hay Street. Here they made a really fine picture, and, keeping good time, the fours properly dressed, the men marched as if on parade. With this exception—they were very noisy. They informed all and sundry what they thought of the camp and of the new regulations. Round into Elizabeth-street and back to the station again, and then the soldiers junctioned with another body of strikers.

Near one of the Elizabeth-street approaches to the station was the 'Pomona' fruit stall. One of the soldiers made for it, another followed, and in a few seconds the stall was surrounded by a surging mass of riotous soldiery. All the fruit was taken—and the soldiers spared nothing of the vehicle to get it. The men started to pelt the big crowd that was watching the proceedings from the balcony of the station and one of the tramway bridges. Oranges, peaches, bananas, all flew about, but misses were more frequent than hits.

The soldiers, still in fours, then proceeded to the fruit stalls at the other end of the station. One soldier made to help himself to the contents of a barrow, but he was so fiercely attacked by the boyish-looking proprietor that he was driven off. Then an AMC non-commissioned man jumped up on to a barrow and started to harangue the men. He exhorted them to play the game, to give the barrowmen a chance, and to get going again. His words had effect. The stalls were left alone, the men formed up and re-commenced their 'protest' march.

Some of the men started to commandeer different vehicles. Motor cars, motor bicycles, lorries, drays, on all of these the men deposited themselves without as much as 'with your leave'. However, in the majority of cases, it was tolerated.

Near George-street, Haymarket, the men broke up into two bodies, some following the battalion colours, others the red-flag-topped Union Jack. The followers of the latter set off down George-street. Except for the frequent raids on vehicles, the men were fairly orderly. Their numbers, however, were diminishing rapidly. At every hotel men broke away, and occasionally other batches deserted the ranks.

Police estimated the number in the original marching group to be 3000, but every arriving train from Liverpool brought more drunken recruits. After the march split, one section went west, towards Chinatown, Grace Brothers store, Broadway and Tooth's Brewery. The other marched down George Street and back up Pitt Street via Elizabeth and Macquarie streets, and then started to break up. Some men went west towards Hyde Park and Oxford Street.

Although there were two main marches, the groups were constantly splitting with smaller groups breaking away. The police report and the newspaper reports seem to contradict each other at times about which group was the 'official' one, and what route it took through the city.

All pubs were targets. Men simply invaded and took over the bars. Those publicans who tried to close their doors had them smashed open. One group marched to Tooth's Brewery on Broadway and another ransacked the Queen Victoria Markets. The Regent Street Police Station, the Grace Brothers store in West George Street, the *Evening News* offices in Market Street and the Manly ferry wharf at Circular Quay were all attacked during the afternoon. The sheer weight of numbers meant that police were powerless to stop most of the rioting.

Newspaper reports and official police and court records indicate that there were two elements that worried the authorities and the general public. Hooliganism and public safety was the main worry, but the idea of soldiers having 'workers' rights' was something that concerned the conservative majority and the readership of the *Sydney Morning Herald*, which seems to have wanted to portray the protestors as either 'hoodlums' or 'bolshies'.

At that time the resistance to conscription was being partly led by organisations like the International Workers of the World (IWW)—commonly known as the 'Wobblies'—and there was a general fear of socialism and unionism. The reporter from the *SMH* was cautious about the 'small red flag'. Although mentioning it and implying that it was part of the 'protest', he also covered himself by adding later that 'This small flag was only an advertisement'.

Following the movements of what appeared to be the 'official' group of marchers, the *Sydney Morning Herald* reported:

When they reached Circular Quay, the men were in fair strength.
Here they tried to invade the Manly ferry wharf, but Sergt.
Marshall and four other police who had accompanied the men

over the greater part of the march, planted themselves at the turnstiles, and kept the soldiers away.

From the Quay the men then marched to the Conservatorium outside Government House grounds, and thence to the Domain Gates, where a few minutes 'smoko' was held. The column was now only half its former strength, but it made an effort to take possession of the Assembly Hotel, opposite the Police Headquarters. Sergt. Marshall and his four men were not strong enough to eject them, so a squad of men from headquarters—mostly 'inside' men—came to the rescue. Every soldier was put out of the hotel, and the doors were closed.

The newspaper suggests that the main march reached Circular Quay and headed up Macquarie Street, while the police report states that this group marched down George Street and back up Pitt Street to near the railway. However, most agree that this group heading back south towards the railway appears to have heralded the end of any 'official march'. The whole event apparently then descended into uncoordinated riotous behaviour, drinking and destruction of property.

Meanwhile, the men from the second marching group were rioting near Chinatown and Broadway, in the vicinity of Tooth's Brewery. According to the *SMH* reporter, it was chaotic:

In Castlereagh-street the men took charge of a waggon belonging to Starkey's Aerated Waters Co., and emptied it of all its contents. The bottles and syphons, after they had drunk their contents, were then thrown about the street and at inoffensive people passing. The next victim was a Chinaman, whose handcart was promptly captured and the contents were strewn along the streets.

In Rawson-place the rioters again raided the street fruiterers, and in a few moments the contents of the carts were being fought for amongst themselves. From a brewer's cart a barrel of beer was seized.

One soldier, waving a broom over his head, and hitting out wildly, was arrested at the Broadway and taken to the lock-up.

> Some of his comrades, who still retained the bottles stolen from
> Starkey's, then threw them at the police, one hitting Constable
> Gordon and wounding him to such an extent as to necessitate his
> removal to the hospital.

At first, the police believed the riotous behaviour had been confined to Liverpool. They were surprised to hear the first reports of the trouble in the city of Sydney and, once they realised what was happening, coordination of services was reasonably prompt and efficient. They immediately ordered the cancellation of train services from Liverpool at around 4.30 p.m., which prevented any more recruits joining the fray.

The New South Wales Labor Premier, William Holman, called an emergency cabinet meeting and was kept informed of developments as the afternoon wore on. He also gave police the use of state government vehicles to travel quickly around the city to trouble spots, and told the chief magistrate to order the closure of all hotels in the city of Sydney and the council areas of Redfern, Glebe, Paddington and Newtown. This was done by 7.30 p.m. and all pubs were shut by 8 p.m.

Meanwhile, by 5 p.m. around 500 more police had been summoned to the city from suburban stations and an hour later the army had 1500 troops ready for action. By 8 p.m. 500 armed soldiers had been sent from the camp at the showground to help the police. State Army Commandant, Colonel Ramaciotti, issued an order forbidding the selling of firearms or explosives in the County of Cumberland, which meant the entire suburban area of Greater Sydney.

By now many of the recruits who lived in and around Sydney had started 'melting away'. Those remaining were mostly in groups of several hundred or less. Some civilians, most of them 'larrikins' and troublemakers, had joined them, and they were slowly gravitating back towards Central Railway Station. For many of the recruits, there was no alternative but to attempt to return to Liverpool and Casula camps.

But the die-hards hadn't finished. Just after 8 p.m. one group, estimated at 100 recruits and 300 civilians, attacked Kliesdorff's tobacconist at the corner of Hunter and Castlereagh streets, smashed the shopfront windows and stole cigars. Police arrested the ringleader, and the mob moved on to the Deutsche Club in Phillip Street and smashed some windows. When dispersed by police, they moved south towards Hyde Park.

The official police report states:

> Between this time and 10 p.m. a number of minor disturbances caused by scattered bodies of soldiers took place in the city.

The report then turns to events at Central Railway Station, where an armed guard had been on duty near the eastern entrance. This detachment of regular soldiers had been sent as a picket to maintain order as rioters started to congregate back at the station. Though the report claims the guard was in place from 6 p.m., they had, in fact, arrived at Central Station after 8 p.m. It tells what transpired in a very brief and matter-of-fact manner:

> About 10.40 p.m. this guard was attacked by a mob of 500 Liverpool soldiers throwing bottles and stones and turning the fire hose on them. A revolver is also said to have been fired at the guard. Ultimately the guard fired into the mob with the result that one soldier was killed and six wounded. The leader of the affray was arrested by the military.

The man killed was 26-year-old Private Keefe, of the 6th Australian Light Horse being trained at Casula. The autopsy showed that a bullet entered his right cheek, fractured the lower jaw, tore the jugular vein, and then entered the left shoulder, the collarbone and the shoulderblade.

The inquest into his death shed further light on the exact details of the day and the movement of men from Casula to Sydney. The *Sydney Morning Herald* reported on 1 March:

> Captain Frank Smith, of the A.I.F., stationed at Casula, said that at about 8.45 a.m. on Monday, February 14, about 2500 men

marched without permission, but in an orderly manner, out of camp to the Liverpool camp. Witness 'fell out' representatives from each company, and sent them to the Camp Commandant's office. Their grievances were mainly the additional hours of training. He advised the men not to attempt to force if there was a picket at the gate. Witness, after the men reached Liverpool, persuaded fully 2000 to return to Casula. At 2.30 p.m. about 1000 men left Casula camp without permission, but in an orderly manner, and made straight for Liverpool station.

If Captain Smith's claim, that he convinced 2000 of 2500 to return to Casula, is true, then most of those rioting in Liverpool and later marching in Sydney must have been men from the Liverpool camp.

Also according to Smith, Keefe was one of those 2000 that returned to Casula camp, and also one of the 1000 or so who departed again at 2.30 p.m. and later took a train to the city.

Lieutenant-Colonel Marcus Logan, in command of the military police picket at Central Railway Station, said it was his understanding that Keefe came down from Liverpool with the main body of protestors in the morning, returned to Liverpool during the afternoon and came back to town again at about 5 p.m. He said he personally ordered Keefe, who he seemed to know, or at least recognise by name, to go back to Liverpool around 9.45 p.m., and this order was disobeyed.

Logan's testimony is recorded in the inquest transcript:

Every civilian was compelled to show a ticket before being admitted to the station, and as soon as they were presented the guard escorted them to the departure platforms. When the large body of soldiers arrived no attempt was made to collect tickets from them. This was so as to avoid trouble. Witness bore in mind that the station might be wrecked, and his job was to get the men back to Liverpool . . .

Before leaving the Show Ground witness warned his men not to hit anyone on the head with their rifles . . . He lowered his dignity as an officer on several occasions by going and addressing the crowd as one of themselves. He used every means to persuade them to go away quietly.

He saw deceased on the assembly platform wandering about in a dazed condition, and cautioned him and several others. Witness said to deceased: 'Now, Keefe, get away like a good lad to Liverpool, because there will be trouble here.' Keefe replied: 'I'll please myself,' and finally witness's attention was directed to him by a non-com., who said, 'That man you cautioned is causing trouble again.'

Approaching deceased again, witness remonstrated with him, and said: 'I have already cautioned you twice this evening. Go away to the departure platform, and remain there.' He (Keefe) clapped his left breast coat pocket, saying, 'I've got enough here to give me permission to remain.' Deceased then moved off towards the departure platform.

In his evidence Logan stated that the approach taken by the military police picket was one of 'cajolery' and claimed that he told his 150 men to remember that the mutineers were still their comrades. He said that he made all men with fixed bayonets fall back away from the action to avoid injuring those in the mob.

The rioters outnumbered the military police about four to one and started to push the picket back. Logan ordered his men to charge the rioters using only rifle butts. The few police officers in attendance used batons. A fire hose was then turned on the picket by the rioters and men in the picket were knocked down. Then the first shots were fired by someone in the mob.

There was also a crowd of some 1200 civilians outside the station entrance, which included troublemakers. Some witnesses gave evidence that shots were fired from within this crowd at the picket.

Police Constable Rupert John Bailey gave evidence that:

The crowd were calling the pickets 'scabs' and 'blacklegs', and inviting them to join them. Stones and bottles were thrown. The crowd broke through the eastern archway. The conduct of the crowd was riotous . . . The hose was then taken by three men and fixed to a hydrant. When the order was given for the picket to line up one of the crowd said, 'Don't be frightened, boys; it's only blank cartridges they have'. The order was then given to the picket to load, and for the crowd to stand back from the hose. Keefe and two other infantry men had hold of the hose at this time, when an order was given to fire. The order came from among the picket.

Logan admitted he did not warn the crowd that the picket was about to fire as it was 'not his intention there should be any shooting' and 'the picket fired in self-defence'. He said in his evidence that:

> The mob behaved in a menacing way. A large stone was thrown at me, and hit one of my men in the back. The mutineers were pressing the pickets back gradually, and were using bad language and making threats. I then warned the men that if they did not at once give in and go to the departure platform and cease interfering with the pickets I would take action. They used bad language and I said, 'I will give you while I count three to get off the platform and will give the word charge'. They took no notice and used filthy language. I then gave the word 'charge, and use the butts not the bayonets.' We had not got them fixed at the time. There were a number of civilians urging the soldiers on, so we bowled over some of them. They threw missiles at us, building material, sand and stones which they obtained from the railway, bottles and pickets wrenched off the fence. They then got a fire hose and drove us back. We then made a second charge, and with the assistance of the civil police, we drove them back and got the hose off them and turned it on the mutineers. There was one continual fight. Three of my men had been knocked insensible by bottles, and one was kicked by a civilian.
>
> It was a wild fight, and you could not distinguish anyone: It appeared that we would be driven into the assembly hall, and the whole station wrecked, if they regained possession of the firehose. It was then I gave the order to the pickets to load. I followed with the command, 'Keep your muzzles up, and if you have to fire, fire low.'

My idea in giving these directions was that by firing low, we
would not kill anyone, but hit their legs, and that only one or two
shots would be required to intimidate them . . . The pickets saw
a man on one knee firing. It was Keefe that was firing. The picket
in self-defence fired. We fired about 25 shots, and the crowd
cleared out. Keefe and my man who was down were dragged into
the refreshment room. Keefe died there. If we had charged with
fixed bayonets instead of firing hundreds of lives would have been
sacrificed. The attitude of the picket was cajolery, as it was known
that Keefe was mad with drink.

The inquest also received evidence from several other police
officers, who more or less backed up Logan's version of events.
Police Sergeant William Bowery testified that:

It was difficult to see what was going on when the shots were
fired, because the lights at the eastern entrance were shot out and
the hose created a dense spray.

Police Constable William Andrews gave evidence that he distinctly
heard the order 'Fire, clear' given by a man in the picket before
they opened fire. Constable Bailey stated that he saw Keefe fall
and went and picked him up and carried him to the refreshment
room, where he died.

It seems apparent that Keefe was very drunk and belligerent.
He certainly helped turn the fire hose on the picket and was in
possession of a pistol, although the weapon was never found. His
mother, who said that he was a good lad who had spent time as an
overseer on plantations in the Solomon Islands and was engaged
to be married, also testified that he took his pistol to camp and
practised target shooting with it.

The coroner's report found that:

The deceased, Ernest William Keefe, died from the effects of
a bullet wound in the head, justifiably inflicted upon him by a
military picket, then in the lawful execution of their duty in

maintaining the public peace and suppressing a riot of mutinous soldiers and civilians.

During the Valentine's Day Riot more than 100 men were taken into custody, and 37 who were arrested and charged by police subsequently came to court. The army court-martialled 280 men.

Private Jack Sutcliffe and Private Frederick Short were accused of leading the parade from Casula. The official charge was 'joining in a mutiny' and they were tried before a General Court Martial on 27 March 1916. Both pleaded not guilty. The court martial was told that Sutcliffe, aged 26, led the recruits' march from Casula camp to Liverpool, while Private Short urged others to join in.

Sutcliffe was found guilty and 'discharged with ignominy' from the army. Sentenced to three years in prison, he served one year, in Long Bay and Goulburn gaols, before being released.

Private Frederick Short turned out to be sixteen-year-old Frederick Nathaniel James, who had enlisted under a false name and lied about his age. He gave evidence that 'a big crowd . . . nearly all the camp . . . was going from tent to tent pulling people out'. He said they ordered him to 'come with us'. In spite of his evidence he was found guilty and sentenced to 60 days' detention.

Another sixteen-year-old, Private William Roy Heaton, was tried at Sydney Quarter Sessions and found guilty of 'maliciously injuring a plate glass window at the Grace Bros department store worth £10' on 2 March 1916. He was sentenced to six months with hard labour.

*The Mirror of Australia* newspaper took up Heaton's case after their court reporter heard his evidence. Heaton was an orphan who supported his younger sister from his army pay. Although sentenced to six months in Goulburn Gaol, the newspaper's campaign saw him released on special licence after ten weeks.

Heaton wrote to *The Mirror*:

Dear Mr Editor,—I am not much of a scholar, so you must not mind if this letter is short. I have to thank 'The Mirror' for taking up my case, and securing my release, and I hope now that I shall be allowed to re-join the Light Horse and get to the front. That is where I want to be, with the boys in the trenches.

Heaton, however, had been 'discharged with ignominy' from the AIF upon his release from jail. So, on 30 June 1916, he re-enlisted as 'William Westacott', served throughout the remainder of the war and only confessed his real identity when he felt it 'safe' to do so, in February 1918.

Many of the men sentenced and 'discharged with ignominy' did the same. Men such as Cecil Madden, who was found guilty of riot at the Central Police Court and sentenced to three months at the Darlinghurst Detention Barracks. He was discharged on his release in May 1916, but re-enlisted five months later, in November 1916, and was killed in action in France in 1918.

At least the army acted quickly, for once, in the wake of the riot. On 25 February, a mere ten days after it reported on the riot, the *Sydney Morning Herald* informed its readers that:

> The Premier was informed yesterday by the State Commandant that by March 9 next the number of men in camp at Liverpool would be reduced to 6000. The number there at the time of the recent riot was 14,000. The Commandant also said that the despatch of men overseas and to the various country camps was proceeding actively.

———

The most far-reaching result of the riot was felt a few months later, and it would change the life of every citizen of New South Wales for the next forty years.

Back on 30 November 1915 James Mitchell, Inspector General of Police, wrote in his official report of the 'disturbances' at Liverpool the previous day:

> It is suggested by the local Police that steps be taken to close the hotels at Liverpool at 6.00 o'clock p.m. while the war continues. This matter comes directly within the province of the military authorities and no doubt will receive their earnest consideration.

After the Valentine's Day Riot, there was no need to wait for the military authorities to act. When the residents of New South Wales had the chance to make the decision four months later, on 10 June 1916, they overwhelmingly voted that pubs would close at 6 p.m. every day, not at 11p.m.

Although there were six choices—each hour from 6 p.m. to 11 p.m.—and despite the liquor industry heavily campaigning for a compromise vote for 9 p.m., a stunning 63 per cent voted for six o'clock!

Thus, New South Wales was condemned to 40 years of the wretched social consequences of the 'six o'clock swill'. Men guzzling down beer after beer after work, and tiled pubs with no furniture being hosed out at 6.30 p.m. Men staggering home drunk, vomiting on the pavement, marriages ruined and home life made a daily torture for many women.

At the same time, crime and corruption spiralled out of control as the supply and trade of booze and 'sly grog' at night was simply handed over to criminals—who added drugs and prostitution and made their fortunes.

As it turned out, the social disorder of 6 p.m. closing time was a terrible price to pay for the riot caused by a few thousand would-be servicemen who were upset about their camp conditions. The Aussie male culture of daily boozing after work was still deeply entrenched long after the law was changed in 1955.

*Footnote:*
Some men stationed at the Casula camp were able to avoid the whole event.

Those lucky enough to have an officer like Patrick Gordon Taylor could be grateful that they were kept right out of the affair. Second Lieutenant Taylor, always known as 'Bill' and nineteen at the time, took his men on a route march along the Holsworthy Road and into the bush. Years later he recalled:

I didn't want my chaps swept up into this shambles. So I lined them up on the parade . . . and told them what I thought was going to happen. I then told them we were going to march out immediately into the country on a skirmishing exercise, and that any man who wanted to stay and join the mutiny must fall out now and leave the company. There were a few sideways glances, but not a man moved.

Taylor's company thus avoided the whole incident.

Later in the war, Bill Taylor joined the Flying Corps, and afterwards he became an aviation pioneer. During the 'Jubilee Flight' across the Tasman in 1935 with Charles Kingsford Smith, Taylor was the man who walked out on the wings of the *Southern Cross* several times to transfer oil from the one 'good' engine to the one that was overheating, thus saving the lives of all three men on board. He was knighted in 1954.

# LINES ON ALE

**Edgar Allan Poe**

Fill with mingled cream and amber,
I will drain that glass again.
Such hilarious visions clamber
Through the chamber of my brain.
Quaintest thoughts, queerest fancies
Come to life and fade away.
What care I how time advances;
I am drinking ale today.

# THERE'S A PATRON SAINT OF DRUNKS

**Jim Haynes**

> 'Alcohol is a very necessary article . . . it makes
> life bearable to millions of people who could
> not endure their existence if they were quite
> sober.'
>
> George Bernard Shaw, 1907

There's a patron saint of drunks. Someone looks after them.

It's almost impossible for a drunk to hurt himself and it's very difficult to get the better of a drunk.

I'm not talking here about part-time drunks or weekend drunks. I'm talking about genuine drunks, those who make a vocation of being drunks, whose character is defined by the fact that they're drunks. We had a few like that in my little hometown of Weelabarabak but the most memorable of them all was the 'town drunk' for many years, Dipso Dan.

His real name was, I believe, Daniel Harvey. The whole town, however, referred to him as 'Dipso Dan', and to his face he was called either just 'Dan' or 'Dipso'.

Dipso Dan wasn't born in Weelabarabak. Like many town drunks he drifted in from somewhere else, found a place to camp, did a bit of casual work now and again and got on with the job of being the town drunk. It was rumoured that he had grown up in Melbourne and come to the bush as a sideshow worker. He'd even fought in boxing tent shows many years ago and was 'pretty handy' according to some of the older blokes around town. Old Nugget reckoned he remembered him going a few rounds with some locals many years ago at the Weelabarabak Show, when he was a regular member of King Riley's Travelling Boxing Show.

As the grog slowly got to Dipso, he slipped down the carnival pecking order, becoming a rigger and a 'rousie' and eventually, when he couldn't perform any regular productive work, he had been left behind in Weelabarabak to become our town drunk.

Dipso wore old woollen army pants tied with rope in place of a belt, a flannel shirt of an indeterminate shade and shoes that varied in type and colour depending on charity. I remember that he never wore socks and his old army pants ended about six inches above his shoes, revealing a fair bit of bony shank.

He was always accompanied by his dog, Digger.

Dipso was a fairly happy drunk, though he could be an absolute pain in the neck if you were trying to have a couple of quiet ones and a bet at the Tatts on Saturday. He always tried to tell you yarns about his illustrious punting career and wanted to know if you had 'a good thing in the next'. But there was no malice in Dipso; he wasn't a 'fighting drunk' in spite of his reputed past career in the ring.

He was painfully thin and seemed incredibly uncoordinated for an ex-boxer. He moved with a strange, jerky dancing motion that I found fascinating when I was a kid. Perhaps it was a combination of his boxing days dancing around the ring and the effect of years of booze.

One year the famous Tintookie Marionette Theatre came to Weelabarabak and put on a show. The whole school was marched down to the CWA hall and sat on mats at the front, near the stage, while the adults who weren't working sat in chairs behind us. The show was a ripper too, although I don't remember the plot or the characters very well. What everyone in town does remember is what happened when the curtain opened.

The first marionette, a swaggie character, appeared on stage. The strings that operated the puppet gave it that jerky walking action that marionettes have. Half the kids on the infant and junior school mats called out in unison, 'It's Dipso Dan!' It almost brought the show to a standstill.

The poor puppeteers must have wondered what these kids were yelling about. They no doubt also wondered why the adult audience was in stitches before the action had even begun. I bet they thought we were a very odd lot and were pleased to move on to the relative civilisation of Cooper's Junction for their evening performance.

Us kids used to imitate Dipso quite a bit, especially after we saw the marionette theatre performance. Kids are pretty insensitive and cruel, and although Mum warned us that it was wicked to make fun of drunks like old Dan, my cousin Gerald and I used to pretend to be Dipso whenever we had creaming soda, a soft drink that developed a creamy head like beer if you shook it up before pouring it.

Weelabarabak had two pubs, the Tattersalls and the Royal. The former was the domain of the Regan family and was run in my childhood by Doug Regan; it was the preferred watering hole for the town's more respectable citizens.

The Royal was run by an ever-changing parade of managers but was ruled over by the toughest woman in town, Dot McPherson, known to all as simply 'Dot the Barmaid'.

Dipso was always getting barred from the Tatts. He had even been barred from the Royal a couple of times, which was pretty rare. He didn't mind that too much; publicans changed fairly regularly at the Royal and they were always desperate for customers, so Dipso wasn't usually barred for long. What did terrify Dipso was the thought of being barred from the Royal by Dot while he was still barred from the Tatts by Dougie.

Dipso lived in mortal fear of Dot, who worked most of the evening shifts at the Royal. If he was barred by Dot he had to rely on getting a sneaky drink from Happy Harold, the barman at the Royal. Harold mostly worked afternoon and weekend shifts.

Dipso's evenings would be very dry and lonely affairs if he was barred from both pubs. It was rumoured that, under these circumstances, Dipso drank metho down in his camp near the river.

I know for a fact that this was more than a rumour because of a conversation I had with Dipso one Friday afternoon at the Tatts. I must have caught him at the very start of a bender because he was quite articulate.

'How's a boy?' he asked. Dipso always slurred his words slightly and his head, arms and shoulders were never completely still when he spoke. You got used to it after a while but it could be very disconcerting at first. He also spoke with a constant slight hesitation that never quite became a stammer. 'Got a winner for t . . . termorrer?'

'No, Dan, haven't even had a look at the form yet,' I answered.

The trick was to be polite, not make eye contact, and hope he'd move on. It worked maybe one time in every three, but not that afternoon.

'Well, you t . . . tell me when you've p . . . picked one,' he said, patting me on the shoulder. 'And how about making an old digger happy and buying me a drink?'

'You're not an old digger, Dan,' I replied, trying to keep my head in the paper.

'I know that,' Dipso chuckled, 'but I got a d . . . dog called D . . . Digger and he'd be happy if you bought me one.'

He could be quite witty sometimes.

So I bought him a seven-ounce glass of beer and he told me about his recent troubles with Dot and Dougie. 'Trouble was I think I p . . . peed me pants on the carpet and Dougie hates that,' he confided to me. 'I'm glad he's let me back in anyhow, a man could end up drinkin' metho!'

'Well, Dan, things aren't that crook yet,' I said. 'Anyway, I don't know how anyone could actually *drink* metho.'

'Well it's not easy,' he replied, 'you need a t . . . terbacca tin and you pour it in real shallow and mix it with condensed milk or s . . . soft drink, cordial mix, or boot polish if that's all you've got, then you can usually get it down.'

I was stunned by the matter-of-fact nature of this reply. 'Strewth, that sounds bloody awful, Dan!' I said.

'Well it t . . . tastes worse than it sounds too,' he assured me, 'but it's even worse if you've got nothing to go with it, then you have to light the fumes and drink it out from under them—straight from the t . . . terbacca tin.'

Dipso went on to tell me all the names metho had when mixed in different ways. It was 'white lady' when mixed with condensed milk, 'red' was the boot polish mix—and there was more that I've forgotten and thankfully never needed to remember!

That conversation changed my attitude to Dipso Dan. I didn't mind buying him the occasional beer once I knew something about the alternatives. I even offered him a lift home once or twice, but he told me he was 'orright' and said the police sergeant usually got him 'back to camp' if he couldn't manage it himself.

Dipso's camp was an old shack down on the river just out of town. Between 'benders' in town he lived there with Digger. Dipso told me dogs were great to talk to when you were drunk and 'no other bastard would talk to you'. He had Digger from when I was a teenager until long after I left town. Digger was a little brown kelpie that Old Nugget Brady had given him as a pup. He was out of Nugget's good working bitch but was the runt of the litter, so Nugget gave him to Dipso for two reasons. Firstly, Dipso had just lost his previous dog to a brown snake down at their camp. Secondly, it meant Nugget didn't have to 'hit the poor little bugger on the head'—Nugget was very soft-hearted for an old bushman.

Digger followed Dipso everywhere and always waited for him outside the pub. Digger was much more popular around town than his master. All the kids would pat him as they passed the pub and my Uncle Lennie used to feed him regularly at the back of the fish and chip shop.

At least Digger ate regularly. Dipso wouldn't eat at all when he was on a bender. Sometimes he didn't get home for days at a time. He'd sleep in Anzac Park or at the back of whichever pub he got thrown out of at closing time, with Digger to keep him warm. If someone caught him up and about before the pub opened, Dipso might be offered something to eat. I think Uncle Lennie fed him occasionally at the back of the fish and chip shop, as well as Digger. Mostly, though, he'd drink for days at a time and then either get some provisions at the general store (a few loaves of bread and tins of camp pie which he'd share with Digger) and go home to dry out for a while, or he'd put himself in the lock-up, if the sergeant hadn't already put him in there for being drunk and disorderly.

Often Mrs Sayer, the police sergeant's wife, would discover Dipso in the cell when she went to clean up in the morning. 'Did Bill put you in there or did you put yourself in, Dan?' she would ask.

'I put meself in, missus,' Dipso would reply, 'I'm real crook too.'

'Well you can have some lunch now and a proper meal tonight, but you're out in the morning,' she'd reply, matter-of-factly.

'Orright, Missus Sayer, thanks,' Dipso would say politely. 'Can you give Digger a feed too, please?'

It was mostly observing Dipso Dan that led me to believe there's a patron saint of drunks. He was indestructible. I've seen him fall down on the concrete outside the cafe and not even drop his shopping. I've seen him fall over the pub verandah at the Royal without breaking the two bottles of beer he had wrapped in brown paper. He would stagger erect in one jerky movement and continue on his wobbly pilgrimage as if nothing had happened.

The other amazing thing was that you could never get the better of him. I remember Dougie calling the sergeant to remove him from the Tatts one night when he'd been particularly obnoxious. Big Bill Sayer appeared within minutes and, filling the door of the pub in his police uniform, said, 'C'mon, Dan, you're coming with me. You drink too much!'

Dipso didn't miss a beat, 'Don't be s . . . silly, sergeant,' he slurred, swaying on the spot, 'you can't!'

My favourite Dipso Dan story concerns the time he supposedly backed a winner with the SP bookie and made a real nuisance of himself until Dougie threw him out of the Tatts. Eddy Pierce's cab was parked outside and Dipso jumped straight in. With his mind totally befuddled by booze, he told Eddy he wanted to go to the Tatts for a drink.

'We're at the Tatts now,' replied Eddy.

'Strewth, so we are!' yelled Dipso, fumbling in his pocket and staggering out of the cab. 'Here's your money and you shouldn't drive so bloody fast!'

As I wasn't there when that happened, I can only assume it's true. I've seen Dipso do some pretty funny things. I can see him now, in my mind's eye—weaving and bouncing jerkily along the main street of Weelabarabak, talking non-stop to Digger as he goes. And the more I think about him and that crazy dancing motion of his, the more convinced I am that there's a patron saint of drunks. Perhaps it's Saint Vitus.

# TIM DOOLEY

## Thomas E. Spencer

Tim Dooley lives down near the end of the town,
With his wife, and a horse, and a dray;
He'll fetch you a cartload of wood for a crown,
Or he'll go out to work by the day;
As a rule, Tim is one of the mildest of men,
And he drinks nothing stronger than tea,
But now and again something happens, and then,
Tim Dooley breaks out on the spree;
Then you hear the folks say:
'Quick! Get out of the way,
For Tim Dooley is out on the spree.'
Then we hear a loud yell, that we all know full well,
'Tis a sound like a wild dingo's bray;
And the deafest old man in the township can tell
It is Dooley in search of his prey;
All business stops, for the folks close their shops,
Women snatch up their children and flee,
And the Methodist parson with fear almost drops,
When Tim Dooley gets out on the spree.
Our policeman turns pale,
And stops inside the gaol,
When he knows Dooley's out on the spree.
Now, the dread of a fray would not cause this dismay,
Or give rise to such panic and fear,

But who can his courage or valour display,
When he feels his last moment is near?
When Dooley gets tight he is mighty polite,
Wants to kiss everyone he may see,
And a whiff from his breath causes sure, sudden death,
When Tim Dooley is out on the spree;
So we hide, or we fly
When the rumour goes by,
That Dooley is out on the spree.

# THE FINAL MEETING OF THE BOOK CLUB

**Jacqueline Kent**

> 'One more drink and I'd have been under
> the host.'
>
> Dorothy Parker, 1935

'**W**ell,' said Caroline briskly, 'shall we choose the book for next time?' She paused, waiting for us to answer. When nobody did, she said: 'What about something by—ooh—say, Virginia Woolf?'

Andree, Allison and I stared into our wine glasses. Jo, who was less polite, groaned.

'Not a good idea?' Caroline opened the third bottle, the verdelho Andree had brought, and carefully topped everybody up. 'And why not? Allison?'

Put on the spot, Allison, who liked to keep the peace whenever possible, shrivelled. 'I'm not crazy about Virginia Woolf,' she confessed almost in a whisper. 'I know lots of people think she's wonderful, but . . . whenever I read anything she wrote, I always feel as if someone's going to make me write an essay.'

'Nonsense!' Caroline sipped her wine. 'Virginia Woolf is a classic writer. She speaks to the female condition . . .'

'Oh, for heaven's sake,' interrupted Jo. 'Virginia Woolf only *speaks to the female condition* if you happen to be an overprivileged, neurotic woman who lived in England during the 1930s and spent time with a bunch of other literary neurotics.' She'd said similar things to me before, though perhaps a little more gently.

'I won't argue with you,' said Caroline in a voice of steely graciousness. 'I'll only tell you that you're wrong.'

'Yeah?'

'This is a really nice verdelho, Andree,' said Allison quickly.

'Just tell me why I'm wrong!' Jo glared at Caroline, gulped her wine and refilled.

Pointedly moving the bottle out of her reach, Caroline said: 'Let's not get too upset, shall we?'

'She was a bit neurotic, Virginia, I suppose,' said Andree. 'But a wonderful writer.'

'Absolutely.' Caroline added thoughtfully, 'And such a lucky woman, too. She had a really, really supportive husband.'

'Here we go,' said Jo to me, under her breath.

'Yep,' said Caroline. 'He really helped her. So she could do her work, write those brilliant books. He kept the house running.'

'I see,' said Jo. 'So you reckon that, while old Virginia was working upstairs on her fabulous prose, Leonard was putting out the garbage without being told? Yep, makes sense. And I bet he knew his way round a chop at a barbecue, too.'

'Ha ha.' Caroline took an angry gulp of wine. 'All I'm saying is, not all of us are lucky in that respect.'

The rest of us tensed, avoiding looking at each other. We knew what was coming.

'It's not as if I ask Hugh to do much,' said Caroline in what she clearly thought was a reasonable tone. 'I know he works hard too. It's just . . . I wish he'd help me round the house. Just a bit more.'

'But don't you think most men are like that?' asked Andree. 'Or most men over thirty, anyway? I mean, Bob for instance . . .'

'Bob is a *saint* compared with Hugh,' declared Caroline. 'Anybody is. Even David.'

'Thanks,' said Jo.

'Hugh will never do anything off his own bat,' said Caroline. 'And he has to make a point about everything I ask him. He can't just mow the lawn, paying attention to the borders, like normal people. Oh no, he has to get my nail scissors and a ruler and make sure I see him measuring every blade of grass . . .'

She finished her wine and poured another glass. 'I think it's true. Men are from Mars. God knows I've learned to live with most of the weird things Hugh does, even the way he eats tomatoes, but . . .'

'Speaking of weird,' said Andree quickly, 'have you ever noticed how men always know the latest sports results, even though you know they haven't read the paper or watched TV or turned the radio on? They just *know*.'

'Messages through the ether from Planet Sport,' suggested Jo. We laughed, except Caroline.

'Don't talk to me about sport!' she cried. 'I just want Hugh to spend more time around the house. Is that too much to ask?'

'You're not serious,' said Jo. 'You really want him to stop earning squillions putting up office buildings and spend more time at home? You're always telling us how much you like having your own space when you need it.'

'Thass true,' admitted Caroline. 'But I'd just like him to take more of an interest in what I do, 'stead of going on about his boring sport, sport, sport all the time. He could be more innerested in this book group, 'frinstance. I tried to tell him about the last book we did, by that French writer. Col . . . Col . . .'

'Colette,' said Allison.

'Yup.' Caroline waved her arm, narrowly missing Andree's full glass. 'How come French people only have one name? Mmm? Anyway, I liked that book. It's sooooo romantic. And I told Hugh that she's a writer who really knows the *heart* of a woman. The *heart* of a woman,' she repeated, and her eyes went all misty. 'And you know what he said?' Pause for effect. 'He said he thought Colette was an Argentinian soccer player.'

'That really surprises me.' Allison was beginning to have a little trouble with consonants. 'Hugh's an intelligent man.'

'Ha!' Caroline pulled the cork out of the fifth bottle with a vicious *plok*.

'Well, he is,' said Andree. 'I mean, he reads, goes to movies . . .'

'I'm sure he's a romantic in his own way,' added Allison.

'Pig's arse,' said Caroline surprisingly. 'Lemme tell you what he did the other night. We got out *Casablanca* on DVD, it's my absolutely favourite movie in the whooooole world, it's soooo romantic. And we got to the ending, and it's the very best bit, and I always cry . . .' Her voice wobbled. 'And Hugh said, he actually said, he wished Ingrid Bergman'd get out of the way, so he could get a better look at the Lockheed Electra behind her.'

Jo and I burst out laughing, and kept laughing for a long time.

'S'not funny!'

'Yes it is,' said Jo. 'Come on, Caroline. Lighten up!'

But there was no stopping Caroline. Without taking breath, she launched into a long, passionate description of her husband as one of the ten worst people in human history, who hated Sunday night costume dramas on ABC Television, always went to the bathroom just after she'd announced dinner was on the table and was capable of sleeping in the same bedsheets for a year if she let him.

From time to time, one or other of us tried to deflect her. We might as well not have bothered. Hugh, she said bitterly, screamed with laughter over fart jokes, and sang 'Achy breaky heart' in the shower without being able to remember past the first two lines. And when first introduced to Caroline's parents, he had picked up two prawns from a platter, slid them under his top lip and pretended to be Dracula . . .

On and on she went, the level in the bottle dropping steadily as she spoke. Allison was slumped in her chair, her head in her hands, stirring only long enough to open the next bottle and fill all our glasses. I found the wood grain of the table to be so beautiful I almost burst into tears. Next to me, Andree was in tears because she had decided she was turning into her mother. Jo, her cheek resting on her arm, was drawing little patterns on the table with a wine-dipped finger. After twenty minutes, the only person sitting straight in her chair was Caroline.

'And . . . not . . . only . . . that.' Caroline suddenly spoke very slowly, with enormous emphasis. 'I haven't even got to what he's like . . . in . . . bed.'

'Oh, for God's sake!' I said.

'No!' Caroline held up a regal hand. 'You are my oldest friends. You Have A Right To Know!'

'Please, Caroline,' said Allison.

'I bet you think he's a sex machine. He thinks he's a sex machine. Well ha. And ha again.' She glared at all of us in turn. 'Ha!'

'We don't really want to hear this,' pleaded Allison.

'Yes, you do,' said Caroline. 'I wanna tell you . . .'

Jo suddenly sat up straight. She looked as bleary as the rest of us, but as she took a deep breath, I felt a sense of misgiving.

'Look,' said Jo, 'if you're gonna tell us what sex with Hugh is like, you might as well not bother. We know.'

'Whaddya mean, you know?'

Jo sighed. 'We've all been there, Caroline.'

Andree and Allison both started to giggle.

'Whaddya mean, you've all been there?' Caroline suddenly sounded quite sober.

'Do I have to spell it out?' said Jo. 'We all know, from personal experience, that Hugh is a dud in bed. Now, can we change the subject, please?'

In the terrible silence that followed, Allison poured Caroline another glass of wine.

# OVER THE WINE

## Victor Daley ('Creeve Roe')

Very often when I'm drinking,
Of the old days I am thinking,
Of the good old days when living was a joy,
And each morning brought new pleasure,
And each night brought dreams of treasure,
And I thank the Lord that I was once a boy.
For not all the trains in motion,
All the ships that sail the ocean
With their cargoes; all the money in the mart,
Could purchase for an hour
Such a treasure as the flower,
As the flower of Hope that blossomed in my heart.
Now I sit and smile and listen
To my friends whose eyes still glisten
Though their beards are showing threads of silver-grey,
As they talk of fame and glory,
The old, old pathetic story,
While they drink 'Good luck' to luck that keeps away.
And I hate the cant of striving,
Slaving, planning and contriving,
Struggling onward for a paltry little prize.
Oh, it fills my heart with sorrow
This mad grasping for Tomorrow,

While Today from gold to purple dusks and dies.
Very often when I'm drinking,
Of the old days I am thinking,
Of the good old days when living was a joy,
When I see folk marching dreary
To the tune of *Miserere*
Then I thank the Lord that I am still a boy.

# THE LOBSTER AND THE LIONESS

## Ernest O'Ferrall

> 'The temperate man sees the same world
> always, the proper inebriate finds the world
> never presents the same aspect twice.'
>
> David Ireland, 1971

At eleven o'clock Thomson, who had broken his glasses during a last whirling argument re the chances of the Liberal candidate, was pushed gently out the side door and told to go home.

Instead of taking the barman's advice, he sat on the horse trough, holding the lobster he had bought for his supper wrapped in newspaper, and held an indignation meeting with himself until Sergeant Jones happened along.

'Goodnight, Mr Thomson,' said the sergeant kindly.

Thomson pushed his hat to the back of his head. 'Good evenin',' he returned sulkily.

'Are ye comin' down the street?' ventured the sergeant.

'Cert'nly not!' said Thomson. 'I've lost me glasses, an' me eyesight's 'stremely bad. I can't see what I'm doin'!'

'Well, come along and walk with me. I'll see ye as far as the gate.'

Thomson rose unsteadily. 'I tol' you before I've broken me glasses. Do you mean to 'sinuate I'm *drunk*?'

'I do not!' said the sergeant. 'I never saw a soberer man in my life! But come along now, an' I'll tell ye somethin' I heard today about Prince Foote f'r th' Cup. I'm goin' your way!'

On those honourable terms Thomson condescended to take up his lobster and allow Jones to pilot him gently toward his lodgings.

According to Thomson's reckoning, they had trudged through 283 deserted streets and turned 1834 strange and unexpected corners, when he found they were both standing still on a vacant piece of land, in front of an enormous board with 'For Sale' on it.

'Wasser matter?'

'I heerd a strange sound,' answered the sergeant. 'Be quiet a minit! Maybe we'll hear it agin!'

They waited breathlessly.

A deep, muffled grunt arose close by.

'That's it!' said the sergeant excitedly.

'Somebody's drunk,' sighed Thomson wearily. 'Sailor prob'ly.'

The sergeant snorted. 'No sailor ever made a sound like that! Look, it's gettin' up! Is it a dog? . . . *Run, man! Run for your life!*' he yelled, and ran heavily up a dark lane.

Thomson, swaying on his feet, patted his leg and called encouragingly to the approaching thing, 'Goo' dog!'

Two yellow eyes glowed in the darkness.

'Goo' dog!' cooed Thomson encouragingly, and patted his leg again.

A deep, hungry growl.

'Come on, ole feller. I won't hurt yer!'

The thing with the smouldering yellow eyes came a step nearer, and Thomson cried out in delight, 'By George! That's th' finest mastiff I've ever seen! I'll get him to foller me back to th' boarding-house!' He staggered off sideways, murmuring endearments, and stopping every few yards to flick his fingers or pat his leg. And the escaped circus lioness followed him as if he had been another Daniel.

They went slowly up the long, flat street that stretched away to a plain of burnished silver, the sea. The moon had slipped from her cloud dressing room and was hurrying down the sky like a woman going in search of a policeman.

Thomson staggered on, hugging his lobster, until he reached a lamp-post. Then he sat down, and calling affectionately to the lioness, started to eat. 'Here ye are, ol' boy,' he cooed. A claw hit the lioness on the nose and dropped to the pavement. The beast growled at the indignity but ate the fragment, and licked her chops with evident pleasure.

Thomson methodically dissected the food with his hands and chewed stolidly, occasionally throwing a bit over his shoulder with a mumbled word of encouragement. The lioness sat on her haunches and growled between courses, but accepted the scraps with a sort of eager humility. This went on till the lobster was no more. Thomson then wiped his mouth with the back of his hand, leaned against the lamp-post and closed his eyes. In a minute he was asleep. In another thirty seconds, he gave a long, whistling snore like the wail of a distant siren.

The wild beast, sitting erect like a thing of stone, growled nervously.

Thomson snored again.

The lioness growled angrily.

Thomson awoke with a start. 'Who said that?' he demanded. 'Who denies that Wade's done more f'r th' country than th' blanky Labor party—*eh*?' He turned slightly and beheld the enormous beast. 'Goo' dog!' he cooed. 'Goo' dog!'

Faintly, from the distant sea of city lights, came the clear chimes of a clock, followed by twelve deep, solemn notes. Brother timepieces to right and left answered it like watchful guardians of the hours.

Thomson rose slowly with a look of determination and flicked his fingers. 'Come on, ol' boy! Mus' be gettin' home!' He staggered along for about twenty yards, and the lioness, her head down and her tail straight out, tracked him step by step. Then he paused. The beast stopped dead, with her glowing, yellow eyes fixed on his face. Thomson didn't notice her; his mind was grappling with some tremendous problem. 'Where did I leave it?' he moaned at last. 'I'll go back an' look!' With tremendous care, he steered a wavering course back to the lamp-post, moored himself to it, and peered all round the circle of light. The thing he sought was nowhere to be seen. 'Dammit! I wonder where I lef' that lobster? . . . I'm certain I had it—an' I can *smell* it now! . . . Somebody's done me for it!'

Far up the street, approaching boot heels made a clear, crisp clatter in the still night. 'I'll ask this chap if he's seen it!' murmured Thomson, and took a firmer grip of the post.

The lonely pedestrian came up rapidly and proved to be a slight young man in evening dress.

Thomson raised his hat. "Scuse me, did you notice a 'stremely large lobster as you came 'long?'

The stranger stopped dead, stared past Thomson into the gloom beyond, and, with a muffled cry of horror, turned in his tracks. He ran with amazing swiftness into the night.

'Hol' on!' yelled Thomson after him, but there was no answer, merely the sound of a man running.

The lobster-loser turned disconsolately and found the lioness looking intently in the direction the stranger had taken. 'Served him right if I sooled th' dog on him!' he reflected bitterly. Then, with an air of resignation, 'Come on, Carlo, ol' boy; if coffee stall's open, I'll get a pie.' Once more he set sail, and the immense beast of prey followed stealthily in his footsteps at a distance of three paces.

Down the road they went, round two corners and across an unoccupied grassy lot, then along a dark, shop-lined street. At the far end near the kerb gleamed the headlights of a coffee stall. As Thomson drew near the proprietor was seen leaning on the counter, absorbed in reading, by the light of his big lanterns, the account of the previous night's fight.

Out of the darkness a command came to him: 'Hey! Give's a pie an' 'nother f'r th' dog!'

The proprietor looked up cheerily. 'Right-oh!' He put down his paper and turned to fill the order. As he opened his oven door a delicious whiff of hot meat perfumed the frosty air. The lioness in the shadow growled loudly.

"Oo did *that*?' asked the hot-pie man suspiciously.

'Sorright,' Thomson assured him, 'th' dog won't hurt yer.'

'Wot sorter dorg *is* it?' persisted the pie man, vainly endeavouring to see what species of animal was beyond the light.

'Mastiff,' explained the amateur lion-tamer wearily. 'Prize mastiff—mos' 'fectionate beast. Gimme two pies!'

The pie artist extracted two of his finest works from the oven and placed them on the counter just as the lioness growled hungrily again.

'Better give us another pie f'r th' dog,' said Thomson, putting a shilling down on the counter, and taking up one of the bandboxes of nourishment.

The coffee-stall man ignored the order, and, leaning far over the counter, looked into the shadow. His eyes bulged with apprehension.

'*That* ain't no mastiff,' he breathed at last. 'It looks more like a—*gorstruth*!' With one mad bound he was over the counter and away. Thomson howled after him indignantly, and waited for five minutes to see if he would come back.

He didn't.

At last, Thomson climbed carefully over the counter, threw two sizzling pies to the lioness, and recommenced on his own. Fortunately the lioness's share fell into the gutter, and was thereby cooled, otherwise tragedy would probably have happened then and there.

After the light refreshments had been consumed, Thomson climbed down and invited Carlo to follow him again. Some blind instinct guiding his feet, he at last came by devious ways to the terrace house where he wasn't a star boarder.

Hanging on to the frost-cold railings in the moonlight, he communed with himself thus: 'If I take th' dog roun' back, I'll wake up all th' dogs in th' place and fall over th' dust-bin. Let's see! . . . Yes, I better take old Carlo in fron' door and go through th' house. That's it! That's what'll do. Come on, ol' chap!'

With extreme care and patience he at last found the keyhole and flung wide the door. Then he lit a match and cooed encouragingly, but in vain, until the flame burned his fingers.

'*I'll* get him in!' he muttered, and, stumbling through to the kitchen, he found a large piece of raw steak. After opening the back door, he returned to the front and waved it at the lioness.

'Come on, Carlo!' he commanded. The beast, growling slightly, started to follow him. He backed into the hall, intending to lure his prey right through; but she was too quick for him. At the foot of the stairs she darted forward and snatched the steak from his outstretched hand.

'Give it here, damn yer!' he hissed, and made a wild grab at the goods.

The brute snarled horribly, and thumped the floor angrily with her heavy tail. Thomson staggered back and his match went out.

A door on the first landing opened explosively, the wavering light of a candle illumined the upper part of the staircase, and a quavering soprano voice cried, 'Is anyone there?'

'Sorright. It's only me!' replied Thomson irritably. 'I've gotter dog!'

The candle, a wrapped-up head and a long thin arm appeared over the banisters. 'Do you mean to say you are bringing a dog through the *house*, Mr Thomson?'

'It won't hurt th' damn house!' retorted the bringer-home-of-lions, staring upward defiantly.

'Mr Thomson,' chattered the partially hidden landlady, 'you are not in a fit state to argue. I will speak to you in the morning!' The hand that held the candle shook with rage, and, as a natural consequence, the light wavered considerably.

'I *am* fit t' argue, and I *will* argue 'slong as I please! An' what's more, I'll do what I damn well please in th' rotten house, and bring as many dogs as I want inter it! Why, yer know yerself it's only fit f'r dogs! Come on, Carlo, ol' chap!'

He made a grab at the lioness's head but missed. The brute snarled again, louder than the largest-sized dog.

'If you have any respect for yourself,' wailed the landlady, 'I say if you have any *respect* for yourself, you will take that bloodthirsty brute out of the house!'

'Gorrer bed!' shouted Thomson. 'Gorrer bed, an' mind yer own bizness, you—you *ole meddler*!'

'How *dare* you!' shrieked the landlady, and fled horror-stricken to her room.

Then, alone and unseen in the hall, Thomson performed a really fine taming feat. Lighting his second-last match to see what he was doing, he walked behind the lioness and gave her a hearty kick. '*Gerrout!*' he yelled and the lioness, with an ugly shriek, ran lightly down the hall and out into the yard. Thomson then shut both doors, back and front, and stumbled heavily upstairs to his room, where, without troubling to undress, he climbed solemnly into bed.

On the stroke of three he awoke and muttered, 'Warrer! I wonder if warrer-bottle's been filled.' He struggled sadly out of bed, and blinked at the wash-stand, dimly visible by the light of the waning moon. He could not make out a water bottle, but something white and round like a china bowl gleamed invitingly by the wash-basin. 'I dunno what's in it, but I'll drink it, whatever it is!' he sighed, and made dry-mouthed for the waiting refreshment. He seized the bowl, and conveyed it halfway to his lips, then dashed it to the floor. It bounced lightly under the bed. '*Blast th' collar!*' he shouted, and started to fumble for matches. He persevered nobly until the water-jug meanly bumped against his elbow and smashed with a terrific sound on the floor.

'That settles it!' he said, and plumped down on the bed. 'I'm not goin' t' degrade meself by gettin' drink for meself in soap-dish!' For five wrathful minutes he sat and savagely wondered how best to revenge himself. Finally he opened his room door and bawled: 'Where's my shavin' water?'

The landlady's door flung open and she appeared on the threshold, done up like a sort of original mixture of Lady Macbeth and the Worst Woman in Sydney after a gas explosion. 'How *dare* you?' she cried tragically. 'What do you *mean* by asking for shaving water at this hour?'

Thomson, not at all abashed, lurched to the lobby railings, and leaned over like a candidate addressing an election crowd from the balcony of an hotel. 'What do I want *warrer* for? *I'll* tell yer why! *I want t' drink it!!* I've decided t' reform and join th' No-Licence crowd. I'm goin' t' be a Wowser! I think pubs are curse to *ev'ry* man! If there were no pubs, you'd have t' keep beer in th' house, and we wouldn't have t' go *out* f'r it. D'ye understan' that, missus? D'yer see?'

'You forget yourself, sir!' trumpeted the landlady.

'I wish *you* wouldn't forget t' put warrer in my room! It's all damn fine t' gas 'bout 'totalism, but why don't you s'ply some warrer? Has warrer gone up?'

'This is too much!' wailed the wretched landlady.

She turned and tapped sharply with her bony knuckles on the door of the next room, and a sleepy male voice said: 'All right! Be there directly.'

Thomson leaned far over the railings and sniffed suspiciously. His nose wrinkled in disgust.

'Who's keepin' bears?' he demanded excitedly at last. 'I'm not goin' t' stay in this place if you're goin' t' take in bears!'

'You are drunk!' chattered the landlady furiously. 'How *dare* you say there are animals in the house?'

Thomson sniffed again. 'Why, th' house stinks like a circus! It's bears, or tigers, or somethin'!'

The landlady raised a shaking hand, and pointed an accusing finger at him. 'If there is anything in the house you brought it in yourself!' she intoned.

The door of the other room opened, and a tall, thin spectacled man, in a purple dressing-gown, stepped out. 'What is all the noise about?' he inquired bitterly, holding his candle on high like the Torch of Liberty.

'I say that there's *bears* in th' house!' repeated Thomson.

The tall man inhaled deeply. 'There certainly is a strong odour of animals,' he remarked acidly.

'What did I tell yer?' cried Thomson triumphantly. His voice rang through the house, and two more doors were heard to open slightly.

The tall, embittered man turned to the landlady. 'I suppose, Mrs Tribbens, Mr Thomson has brought home a monkey or something of the kind. He seems to be able to do just as he pleases in this house. I dare say we shall become used to the smell in time; but I really must object to being called up in the middle of the night to talk about the matter. Surely it would have done in the morning!'

'You don't understand, Mr Pyppe,' retorted the landlady with fearful hauteur.

'No, I'm afraid I don't,' said Pyppe irritably. 'The whole thing seems ridiculous to me. Why on earth I should be called out of bed at this hour of the night to talk about an unpleasant smell with a man who is obviously . . .'

*Crash!* The tinkle of glass falling on stone told the landlady that the kitchen window had succumbed.

'*What's that?*' she gasped. Down the pitch-dark hall they heard sounds which suggested a burglar in stockinged feet dragging the body of a murdered boarder over the linoleum.

'I will see what it is!' Pyppe announced in a loud voice, and went cautiously downstairs, a step at a time.

Thomson and the landlady stared after him.

'*Who is there?*' cried the brave investigator, holding his candle far out over the railings.

There was no answer.

'*Who is there?*' he snapped. His candle tilted and a drop of hot wax detached itself and fell into the well of gloom. A grating, bestial roar of rage rang through the place, and a lithe, yellow animal sprang into the lighted radius and stood lashing its tail.

'*My God, it's a lioness!*' shrieked Pyppe, really shaken for the first time in his life. His candle clattered from his hand, and he rushed upstairs into his room and slammed and bolted the door.

'I *tol'* yer so!' shouted Thomson exultantly outside the landlady's door, from behind which came hysterical sobs and the shrieking of castors. 'I *tol'* yer there was bears in th' house!'

'The police!' wailed the distracted woman. 'The telephone! Ring for the police!'

'I give you me notice now,' continued Thomson, above the sounds of hurried barricading. 'I think it's disgustin'! *Why, your damned lion might have eaten my dog!* I'm going t' leave t'morrer, d'ye *hear*? I'm not goin' t' live with lions! I'm *sick* of yer stinkin' house!'

A deep, menacing growl floated up the staircase.

Thomson sprawled over the rails. '*Shurrup!*' he commanded, and the lioness, absurdly enough, was still. 'Stinkin' brute!' he muttered without the slightest sign of fear, and made for the telephone on the landing.

In a minute or so he had the police station, and was speaking: 'That th' p'leece station? Yesh. Well, this is Thomson speakin' here. Eh? Yesh, Thomson, of Gladstone Manshuns (*I don't think!*). Can you hear? . . . I say, there's a lion in th' hall here waitin' t' be fed . . . Eh? . . . Yes, a *lion!* . . . No, I'm wrong, ol' chap—it's th' lion's wife. Are you there? . . . Well, it's waitin' t' be fed. I dunno who it b'longs to, but I'm goin' t' leave in the mornin'. It's stinkin' th' place out. Eh? . . . *What's* that? . . . Yesh, Gladstone Manshuns—you know th' place near th' Town Hall! Eh? . . . No, nobody's killed; there's nothin' here t' eat but boarders, never is! Are you comin' along? . . . Right-oh!' The bell tinkled hurriedly in the darkness. Thomson fumbled his way into his room and shut the door.

It was a lovely, peaceful morning. There wasn't a sound until two policemen and a little man, in the ring-costume of a tamer, trotted round the corner.

Thomson waved frantically to them from his window. 'Go roun' side an' get in th' scullery window!' he howled. 'Look out f'r my dog in th' backyard, he's a big mastiff, but he won't hurt yer. If he growls give him a bit o' lobster, he loves lobster!'

# 'DOOGAN'

## C.J. Dennis ('Den')

Doogan's a byword, Doogan's a butt, Doogan's the town
    disgrace:
Loafin' around in his dirty clo'es, down at the heel an' out at
    the toes,
Cadgin' a drink from the fellers he knows, workin' from place
    to place.
Beggin' for work when he's down-an'-out, toilin' a while an'
    then:
Doogan, Doogan, Dithery Doogan, lickerin' up again.
Doogan was once the township's pride; youthful, wealthy
    an' wild,
Free an' easy and devil-may-care, into the thick of it
    everywhere;
With a house an' land and a spankin' pair, an' a beautiful wife
    an' child.
Welcome he was as the flowers in May an' a popular man
    with men;
Doogan, Doogan, Dashaway Doogan, racketin' round again.
Champagne suppers it was them days, horses an' dogs an' sport.
Dashaway Doogan led the dance; Daredevil Doogan took the
    chance,
An' none was there with a warnin' glance, but all to flatter
    an' court.

For Dashaway Doogan called the tune, an' who was to pay
the score.
But Doogan, Doogan, Dashaway Doogan, fillin' 'em up once
more.
He spent his money, he lost his land, he buried his wife an' child
All in the space of a year they say, then Dashaway Doogan
drifted away
With never a sign for many a day, but many's the tale an' wild
They told of his doin's when I was a girl, told with a laugh an'
a sigh,
Of Dashaway Doogan, Drinkin' Doogan, king of the days
gone by.
He came back here when his hair was grey, pinnin' his hopes
to the town,
And hung out a sign as an auctioneer, then agent, wheat
buyer, all in a year.
But none could trust him, because of the beer: an' how could
he go, but down?
Early an' late he was over the way, thick with the drinkin'
men
Doogan, Doogan, Dissolute Doogan, fillin' 'em up again.
Down the ladder he quickly ran, an' how could he hope but
fail?
He drank till he hadn't a coin to spend; he drank till he hadn't
a worthy friend;
He drank till he stole, an' that was the end, an' a couple of
months in jail . . .
Now he's the soak an' the odd-job-man, loafer, rouseabout,
clown:
Doogan, Doogan, Dilly ole Doogan, lowest in all the town.
I often wonder what Doogan thinks as he shuffles along out
there,
Off on his errand of cadgin' beers, passin' his friends of the
early years,
An' some of 'em pities an' some of 'em sneers. But Doogan?
Oh he don't care.

He calls 'em all by their Christian names, George an' Harry
    an' Ben:
Doogan, Doogan, Draggety Doogan, cadgin' around again.
Doogan' failin' in these last years, an' he'll end as all of 'em do,
The fine free fellers who never can save, the devil-may-cares
    who won't behave,
An' they'll rattle him off to a pauper's grave, an' a real good
    riddance too.
With never a sigh for his passin' by, an' never a friend to weep
When Dashaway Doogan, Dithery Doogan, goes to his sober
    sleep.

# THE EVENING BEFORE LEAVING HOME

## 'Steele Rudd'

> 'I rather like bad wine . . . one gets so bored
> with good wine.'
>
> Benjamin Disraeli, 1845

It was drawing close to New Year when Sam Condle sent me word to get ready to go shearin' down the rivers with him an' some other chaps.

I was ready to go anywhere with anyone, not because there weren't plenty work about Vinegar Hill, but because Connie told me straight out one evenin' that she didn't want me comin' to see her any longer. An' after all th' conversation lollies I bought her, an' all th' wood I chopped for her too! By cripes, it made me furious.

'I'm off in th' mornin',' I sez to th' old lady. 'An' might never come back to these parts again.'

'Frankie, if I was you I wouldn't,' she sez, with a terrible sad look on her.

Ah, an' when I think of how she coaxed an' coaxed me to stay, brings the tears to me eyes!

'Me boy, you are not strong enough to shear beside men as old as your father,' she would say, 'so wait till you get set an' have more practice.'

Of course I didn't tell her about Connie, but I quoted Jack Howe shearin' his three hundred a day to her, an' reckoned if I couldn't hack me way through a couple o' hundred I'd eat me hat.

'An' th' terrible floods they have in them rivers,' she went on, 'carries horses an' men away; an' th' wild blacks. Oh, they'll massacre you all in th' night!'

I never heard anythin' before about blacks bein' down th' rivers, an' it made me hair stand up when she mentioned them.

'We'll give them all th' massacrin' they want, mother,' I sez, treatin' it lightly, but at th' same time makin' up me mind to ask Sam how many there was down there.

'An' y' can't go without seein' your father,' th' old lady continued, 'there he is not over his birthday yet. Oh, th' terrible fool of a man that he is, an' gettin' worse instead of better every year. Where he'll find th' money to pay Dollar his wine bill when it's all over, I'm sure I don't know. This is no life for me an' your sisters to be livin', Frankie, an' if you're goin' to go away it will be far worse.'

'He's been down there too jolly long, no doubt about that,' I said, waggin' me head in agreement with her, and appearin' wise at th' old man's expense. 'An' if he ain't home be eight o'clock tonight I'm goin' down to bring him.'

'He might come for you,' the old lady answered with a sigh, 'but if I go near him there'll only be words, an' then he won't come at all.'

When eight o'clock arrived, o' course th' old man wasn't home, an' down I goes to Dollar's.

Near Codlin's corner I sees a light comin' along th' road, an' hears a wheel squeakin', then a cove starts singin' loud an' another chap tells him to 'hold his tongue'. For a while I couldn't make out what sort of a trap they was drivin', but I could tell it was th' old man who was singin' be th' sort of 'cooee' he used to begin the lines with. He always sung like a dingo howlin'. But when we got close together an' I sings out, 'Hello!' they stopped. An' there was th' old man squattin' as comfortable as you like in a wheelbarrow with his back to th' wheel an' his legs danglin' over the back an' a lighted candle stuck on each side of him, an' a big square bottle o' wine in his arms, an' old 'Scottie' nearly as screwed as himself in th' handles of th' barrow.

'By cripes!' I sez to them, 'this is a nice sort o' thing.'

'Thash you, Frankie?' sez th' old man.

'Of course it's me,' I growled at him. 'This is a nice sort of business; an' them sittin' up waitin' for y' at home.'

'Yer needn't go down to (hic) Dollar's for me. I'm comin' home (hic) meself. Ain't we, Scot-(hic)-tie?'

'Aye, comin' home in (hic) Dollar's motor car, d' y' see, Frankie.' An' raisin' th' handles of the barrow, Scottie proceeded to propel th' old man over stones an' ruts at a vigorous and reckless speed again.

I trotted along beside them actin' as a guide, an' thinkin' of the reception they would get from th' old lady when they reached home, an' silently wonderin' if all the horrors of drink wasn't more than compensated for be th' humour of it.

Every hundred yards or so Scottie would stop an' puff hard, an' tell th' old man he was as 'heavy as yon German lassie i' th' wine (hic) shop'.

'Take another drink,' an' th' old man would hold out th' bottle to him. 'An' make me a bit (hic) lighter for yourself.'

Then Scottie would drink, an' off again.

Arrivin' at th' house th' old man broke into fresh song, an' th' dorgs begun barkin' an' th' old lady followed by th' girls come runnin' out. I knew they'd get a surprise when they saw him in th' barrow between th' candles like a blitherin' Chinese god. An' they got one too.

'I've brought him home to y' in a (hic) motor car, d' y' see,' Scottie said to them, stickin' to the handles to keep himself from fallin'.

But they just stood starin' as if they had no tongues to talk with.

Last th' old man who kept blinkin' an' hiccupin' at them, an' thinkin' of th' blokes he saw givin' up their seats to ladies in th' tram th' time he took Fogarty's bull to th' exhibition, opens his mouth an' sez: 'You'll (hic) 'scuse me, ladies, for keepin' me (hic) seat.'

Th' girls an' me bust out laughin', but th' old lady lost her block.

'You beast!' she shouted, an' grabbin' one of th' candles nearly burnt off his whiskers with it. Then she kicked the barrow over, an' th' other candle went out an' old Scottie fell on top of th' old man an' they both started roarin' an' bitin' each other, an' I got ready to run. But seein' th' others wasn't frightent I waited too.

'A lovely pair! Two beautiful specimens of men! Come away, girls, come inside an' leave th' brutes.'

An' carryin' what was left of th' bottle o' wine which she rescued when th' barrow went over, th' old lady bounced inside an' I after her.

Next mornin' first thing I rolled me swag up an' strapped it on th' pack horse along with a jackshay an' a pair o' greenhide hobbles that I made on purpose about three months before.

Soon as breakfast was over I grabs me hat an' sez, 'Well, I got to meet th' rest of th' chaps at Hodgson's Creek in about an hour.'

Then th' hand shakin' an' th' cryin' commenced, which was always the worst part o' going away. Anyone who's never left a home in th' bush don't know what that means.

'Look after y'self, Frankie, while you're away,' th' old man who was the last to shake sez, 'an' if ever ye see any drinkin' or gamblin' goin' on, keep away from it.'

# WONDERFUL LOVE

Anonymous

The wonderful love of a beautiful maid,
The love of a staunch, true man,
The love of a baby unafraid—
Have existed since life began.
But the greatest love, the love of loves,
Even greater than that of a mother,
Is the passionate, tender and infinite love
Of one drunken bum for another.

# THE MIXTURE AS NEVER BEFORE

## Lennie Lower

> 'Be not drunk with wine . . . but be filled with the Spirit.'
>
> Ephesians 5:18

A festive air seems to be pervading the district. The peasantry are warming up in preparation for the usual bout of Christmas and New Year parties. Your poor Uncle Lennie is just getting over a cocktail party, and there is another one looming on the horizon.

I never did care much for cocktail parties. I'm all the time looking for a place to put the olive stones. You can't park them under the table like chewing gum. Cherries are easy; they just go down whole with the drink, toothpick and all.

Just recently I flung a party for Arbuthnot, my grandfather, in celebration of his reaching the age of discretion. Having reached the age of ninety-five, he found that his financial resources were so limited that discretion looked the best shot on the table.

I made the cocktails in the washtubs, and we had a few cases of whisky for the teetotallers. Ever tasted an Angel's Smack? I can mix an Angel's Smack, a Horse's Neck, a Sidecar or a Viper's Breath just like mother used to make. Good stuff, too. You can get happy washing up the glasses.

I had a lot of trouble with the savouries, or horse devours as the French call them. The average hostess's idea of a savoury is

149

to butter a biscuit and plonk a bean on top of it. Some, I'll admit, make such an artistic mess of gherkins, anchovies, chillies and cheese that the whole biscuit is suitable for framing, and only a vandal would eat it. But I invented a savoury composed of a hard-boiled egg and sandsoap. All the guests said it was a wow.

My grandfather came forward with a suggestion for a biscuit soaked in bromide with an aspirin tablet embedded in it. This was one of the few sensible suggestions he made during my preparations for the party.

Have you ever paused in your mad rush to the sideboard and considered what a lot of work has gone into the making of those cocktails and savouries you're wolfing down like a famished greyhound? I spent hours at those washtubs, pouring in this and that: a bit of gin, a dash of bitters, a bucket of absinthe, a handful of curry, my wristwatch (this was unintentional, but I may tell you that after I had fished it out it has been gaining an hour every five minutes, and when I go to put it on it walks away from me) and some stale beer, boot polish and vermouth: French vermouth and Italian vermouth. I wasn't game to put in any Abyssinian vermouth. Anyhow, seeing that both the French and the Italian vermouths were made in Australia, it didn't matter much.

Then I had to boil a copper full of frankfurters, and I had to open tin after tin of *petit poisson* (French, means sardines). Tasted like poisson, too, after I'd finished with them.

When the guests arrived they all hung about like people do at cocktail parties, talking about racehorses and books and pictures and what a rotten hat Mrs Stogers had on, and how Miss Flethers, who was always talking about quarrels with her dressmaker, usually got her frocks at the jumble sale in aid of the Sunday school picnic . . . you know.

Then when the gun went they fell upon my savouries and I was kept busy dashing backwards and forwards to the washtubs and ladling out cocktails. Fortunately I ran short of olives and had to use nutmegs, which seemed to slow them up a bit. There are no stones in nutmegs, by the way. Just thought I'd tell you.

Then Arbuthnot made a speech. We tried to stop him but he threatened to pull the plugs out of the washtubs, so we let him go.

'Ladies and gentlemen,' he said. 'I wish to thank you all for coming here and burning holes in the furniture and eating us out of house and home. As you all know, I have now reached the age of discretion, when I have to live on charcoal biscuits and sterilised dill water. It has taken me years and years to reach this happy state and, believe me, the happiest times of my life were spent in acquiring my present nervous debility, gout, dyspepsia and various duodenal ulcers.'

The guests then pulled him off the piano and locked him in the bathroom. Following which, one of my guests asked me what the devil I was doing hanging about the place, and why wasn't there any music or something, and I got thrown back into the wash-house and told to make more cocktails.

So I put four gallons of prussic acid in the mixture and served it out. They all said it was great and asked for more. That's what cocktail drinking does to your system. Either you succumb after the first few weeks, or you become immune and unpoisonable.

Any of you girls who have a secret yearning for the bright lights had better be warned against cocktail parties. Many an innocent girl has learned to chew gum at a cocktail party, to the utter horror of her parents, who have hurled her out into the snow to battle through life alone and unaided without a soul to care whether she lived or died, and finished up in a squalid tenement scantily clad in filthy rags and dying neglected, with a bag of cocaine clutched in her hand.

There, there, now! I've made you cry! Uncle didn't mean it as bad as that. He just wants you to be warned, that's all. If any dark and handsome stranger approaches you and offers you a cocktail, spurn him. Stick to rum.

# HER DYING WISH

## Anonymous

Shone the moonbeams very faintly
On a face serene and saintly;
On a girl's face like a flower far too fair for long to last,
And their pallid silver fingers—
Lo! how lovingly each lingers!—
Touched her cheeks and told the story she was dying—dying
    fast.
At her bedside stood her lover,
Stood and bent him down above her;
Stricken sore with bitter sorrow, writhing in the clutch of
    grief;
Then she whispered, 'Best and nearest,
Do not mourn for me, my dearest;
I shall soon be up in Heaven, where all pain finds sure relief!
But, before I do forsake you,
I've one last request to make you.'
'Name it, dear,' he said: 'I'll do it if it's in the power of man.'
Then once more he bent above her,
And she whispered to her lover:
'When the funeral takes place, dear, keep as sober as you
    can!'

# SECTION THREE
## PUBS

# THE DRINKERS' HYMN

**Anonymous**

Bless this pub oh Lord we pray,
Keep it open night and day.
Bless the lager and the stout,
Bless the one who serves it out.
Bless the staff of either sex,
Keep them safe from bouncing cheques.
Keep the beer cold when it's hot,
Whether on the slate or not.
Keep the regulars drinking hard,
Reinstate them when they're barred,
And keep them safe, and in thy sight,
When they go staggering home each night.
Bless this pub oh Lord we pray,
Keep it open night and day.

# AUSSIE PUBS

## Jim Haynes

> 'There is nothing which has yet been contrived by man, by which so much happiness is produced as by a good tavern or inn.'
>
> Dr Samuel Johnson, 1776

The English humourist, Willie Rushton, once called Australian pubs 'vast tiled puking parlours'. He was, of course, comparing them to the usually much smaller, cosier British pubs—and he made the comment in the early 1960s, when most Aussie pubs were still designed to cater for the 'six o'clock swill', when large crowds of working men packed into pubs to drink as much as they could between finishing work and the pub's enforced closure at 6 p.m.

Before 1916, when the law was enacted in most of the country and pub architecture changed to accommodate the 'six-o'clock swill', Aussie pubs varied in style, size and design in much the same way as British pubs do. The exception to the copying of British pub designs were the bush 'shanties' which sprung up along coach roads and around the goldfields. These were often unlicensed ramshackle huts of various sizes, with a bar.

As there was a need for basic sleeping quarters for travelling bushmen, and a social centre for the community, the large stately two-storey pubs, with wide verandahs and balconies, became a

feature of many country towns. Luckily many survive to this day.
The best of these pubs also have a breezeway under the verandah,
and perhaps Queensland has the most beautiful examples.

You might think that finding the 'oldest' pub in Australia would
be a simple enough thing. Think again! It's a minefield of different criteria. Do you mean the oldest building? The oldest licence?
The oldest pub name? Or, maybe, the oldest continuously trading
establishment?

Let's start by narrowing the criteria to licensed pubs. There may
well be older pubs that began trading without a licence and then
obtained one at a later date.

The oldest licence still trading belongs to the Woolpack in
Parramatta, which began trading in April 1796. However, this pub
has changed its name several times and at one stage moved across
the road into a different building.

The oldest continuously trading pub in New South Wales is the
Surveyor General in Berrima, which received a licence in 1834, but
the pub in the oldest building is the Macquarie Arms at Windsor.

The building which houses this hotel was constructed in May
1815 after Governor Macquarie had, in 1811, given Richard
Fitzgerald a 'large allotment in the square on the expressed condition of his building immediately thereon a handsome commodious
inn of brick or stone and to be at least two stories high'. Naturally
the owner was delighted at the vice-regal patronage and called
it the Macquarie Arms. Not long after the pub began trading in
May 1815, the governor graced the hotel with his presence and the
*Sydney Gazette* reported:

That spacious and commodious new Inn at Windsor, called The
Macquarie Arms, was opened by the GOVERNOR, on Wednesday
the 26th instant, when HIS EXCELLENCY entertained at
dinner the Magistrates and other principal Gentlemen residing
at Windsor, and in that neighbourhood. Mr. Ransom, who has
taken on himself the duties of Innkeeper, is, from his experience
in the avocation, thoroughly competent to the undertaking,
which we are convinced will be conducted on a liberal footing. Its

necessity has long been manifest as there was no house of public reception at Windsor capable of accommodating large and genteel companies, whereas the Macquarie Arms from its extent, plan of building, and adequate number of apartments will be doubtless found worthy of the most liberal patronage and support.

The licence of the Macquarie Arms has not, however, been continuous and the pub ceased trading for long periods of the building's history.

The Macquarie Arms often claims to be the oldest pub 'on the mainland' because the oldest continually licensed hotel operating on the same site and in the same building in Australia is actually the Bush Inn in New Norfolk, Tasmania. The Bush Inn operates in a building which is as old as the Macquarie Arms, being also constructed in 1815, though the licence was only granted to this pub on 29 September 1825.

New Norfolk was so named because it was the place to which the residents of Norfolk Island were taken when the island was closed as a penal settlement in 1814. Until then the island settlement had operated in conjunction with the one at Sydney. The island was to lie abandoned until 1825 when another, far more punitive and brutal, convict settlement was begun there as the 'last resort' and harshest place of punishment for recalcitrant convicts.

Apparently the relocated residents of Norfolk Island drank illegally in their new home from their arrival in 1814 until the local pub was granted a licence in 1825.

But, what about the first pub, or at least the oldest pub, in the oldest European settlement in Australia, good old Sydney Cove?

Surely we can have a look through those early records and the official government 'newspaper', the *Sydney Gazette,* and find some evidence to proclaim the first pub in Sydney . . .

Sadly, however, it's really a matter, once again, of making up your own set of criteria and then putting in a claim!

The Lord Nelson in Kent Street is a heavyweight contender. On 29 June 1831, Richard Phillips obtained a liquor licence for a pub on the northeast corner of Kent and Argyle streets. It was called the Shipwright Arms but the next year, because of the support of the seafarers and workers on Observatory Hill, he changed the name to the Sailor's Return.

In 1838 Phillips sold the pub to a plasterer, William Wells, who lived on the opposite corner in a two-storey colonial home he'd built in 1836 using sandstone blocks quarried from the area at the base of Observatory Hill. Wells continued to operate the pub opposite his home, firstly as the Sailor's Return then in 1840 as the Quarryman's Arms. A year later he sold the pub and, on 1 May 1841, he obtained a liquor licence for his home, which he then called the Lord Nelson.

The hotel has now been restored with the aid of an 1852 photograph and is often cited as Sydney 'oldest pub', although the licence was not only transferred, it was also not, perhaps, the original licence granted. To make things even more confusing, the current licence was also restored or renewed, or lapsed and was re-granted, at some other point in the pub's history.

Confused? Don't worry, just go and have a drink there, the Lord Nelson is a beaut pub!

Then there's the Fortunes of War in George Street. It was licensed in 1828, and the 1830 certificate of the licence renewal is still on the wall. The pub you visit on the site may well be the oldest continuously licensed public hotel in Sydney but it is not the original building. The current pub was built in 1922 in art nouveau style after a fire destroyed the original. As I said, it depends on your criteria.

We do, however, have a clear claim to the oldest continuously operating pub in the same building in Sydney!

The Hero of Waterloo in Lower Fort Street was built by convict labour in 1843 for stonemason George Paton. If you look at the walls, you can still see the gouges in the rock from when it was heaved out of the ground so long ago. If you look really hard, you can see that the gouges are a consistent pattern on particular stones, but vary from stone to stone. That's because each convict had to meet a certain quota of stones, and the particular cut pattern allowed the convict to identify his stones at the end of the day. The best thing about the Hero of Waterloo, probably because of the stone, is that it's still basically the same pub that it was more than 170 years ago. While most so-called 'old pubs' only have a skerrick of the original building left in them, the Hero is the real thing.

Licensed as a pub in 1845, it was a favourite with the various 'Red Coat' regiments of the British Army that were posted to Sydney throughout the 19th century. So there is a delightful irony in the fact that the Hero these days is known as an 'Irish pub', and employs many Irish staff.

In the pub's early days, just after transportation ended in 1840, the local Irish population was seen as somewhat of a threat to the stability of the colony—more than one third of Sydney's population at the time were Irish born or descendants of Irish convicts or settlers. British regiments were sent to keep order, and they, of course, frequented the Hero of Waterloo, with its very patriotic British name. After all, it wasn't only the rowdy Irish who needed a drink. With its red-coated clientele, the pub certainly would not have been a hotbed of rebellious Irish sentiment back then!

As you can see, Australian pubs originally were often named in the British tradition, i.e. patriotically—after British military heroes or royalty, with monikers like the King's Head, or the Crown, which is the most common pub name in Britain. Sadly, some of the quirkier British pub names rarely appeared on our shores, so let me include here a few of my favourites. The very common Drum and Monkey probably derives from early Victorian times when British pubs used 'drumming monkeys' from the exotic colonies as novelties to attract customers.

There's also the Swan With Two Necks, which is a corruption of 'the swan with two nicks'. Due to an old odd tradition, all swans in Britain were owned by noble families or by various ancient guilds of merchants. Ownership was distinguished by a pattern of cuts in the beak of each bird, and the king or queen could claim all unmarked adult birds. The swans owned by the guild of wine and beer merchants were marked with two nicks in the beak, thus evolved the pub name.

The very odd Elephant and Castle, which is a suburb of South London as well as a common pub name, has had some weird and wonderful stories invented to explain its origin. Among the more ridiculous is that the name is the cockney version of 'infanta de Castille' ('little princess of Castille'), referring to the Spanish princess who became Henry VIII's first wife, Catherine, mother of Mary Tudor. Sadly the story breaks down—Catherine was a princess of Aragon, not the nearby province of Castille!

It's more logical that the name refers to the cutlery factory that originally occupied the site of the first pub called Elephant and Castle. Because the factory made cutlery with ivory handles, it used the image of an elephant with a 'howdah' or covered shelter, vaguely reminiscent in shape of a castle tower, on its back. This elephant and castle was the company's symbol, and the image was used on the sign hanging outside the pub that replaced the factory.

But, back to Aussie pub history.

As time went by in colonial Australia, the pubs were named rather more prosaically than their British counterparts, though many copied British pub names that can still be found here, like the White Horse, the Black Lion, and the Rose, Shamrock and Thistle. Others, like the Macquarie Arms and Surveyor General, seem to have been named in thanks to those who granted the land or the licence.

Some were simply named after their owners, like the famous Young & Jackson in Melbourne, but many more were named from their clientele.

The Sailors Arms, the Ship Inn, and the First and Last are all found near the wharves. The Woolpack was a common name and those pubs would be found where teamsters rested their horses and bullocks, usually near a ford or bridge. The Commercial was often the 'middle class' pub in any country town and had accommodation and smoking rooms designed for commercial travellers.

The Railway, or sometimes the Locomotive, which was always near the station and catered to passengers and railway workers, often became the 'bloodhouse' or rough pub; while the more 'upmarket' pubs, like the Imperial, the Royal and the

Squatters Arms catered to the landed gentry and more conservative drinkers.

Labor voters were more likely to be found drinking at the Australian, the Southern Cross, the Workers Arms or the Railway; while the Tattersalls, Sportsman's Arms, Bat and Ball, and Cricketers Arms catered for sportsmen and gamblers.

Many pubs simply took the name of the closest landmark and were known by such dull names as the Pier, the Bridge and the Lakes.

There are a few pubs that used history to brand themselves as patriotic. Most of these date from colonial times and celebrate British history, like the Trafalgar and Lord Nelson. A special mention must go to the Hero of Waterloo, the Wellington and the Iron Duke—all named after the same bloke!

Pub names do, however, come and go and often lose touch with their original clientele and history. The historic suburb of Botany, in Sydney, is a perfect case in point. Botany has a mix of historic and matter-of-fact pub names. It has the rather obvious Botany Bay and Pier, although the actual pier 'disa-pier-ed' decades ago. Botany also has the local historic connection with patriotic pubs named the Joseph Banks and the Captain Cook.

Until recently Botany also had the Endeavour, but that pub has recently been renovated and reverted to its original name, the Waterworks. It was the pub where the workers from the Botany waterworks and pumping station drank when the nearby 'Millpond', previously known as 'The Botany Swamp', was Sydney's water supply from 1860 to 1888.

It's nice to see some accurate history restored. The crew of the *Endeavour* certainly never drank there. They were too busy drinking Captain Cook's potent fruit punch to prevent scurvy!

# THE LOCAL PUB

## Wilbur G. Howcroft

I must go down to the pub again,
Though you'll surely wonder why,
When all I'll get is some tepid beer
And a musty, tooth-marked pie.
Yes, I must go down to that filthy hole
But the reason's plain, you see,
Though I hate the sight of the lousy dump—
I'm the hotel licensee.

# A BUSH PUBLICAN'S LAMENT

## Henry Lawson

> 'Drunkenness, the fruitful parent of every species of crime, is still the prevailing vice of the colony.'
>
> Sir George Gipps, 1839

I wish I was spifflicated before I ever seen a pub!

You see, it's this way. Suppose a cove comes along on a blazin' hot day in the drought—an' *you* ought to know how hell-hot it can be out here—an' he dumps his swag in the corner of the bar; an' he turns round an' he ses ter me, 'Look here, boss, I ain't got a lonely steever on me, an' God knows when I'll git one. I've tramped ten mile this mornin', an' I'll have ter tramp another ten afore to-night. I'm expectin' ter git on shearin' with ol' Baldy Thompson at West-o'-Sunday nex' week. I got a thirst on me like a sunstruck bone, an' for God sake put up a couple o' beers for me an' my mate, an' I'll fix it up with yer when I come back after shearin'.'

An' what's a feller ter do? I bin there meself, an', I put it to you! I've known what it is to have a thirst on me.

An' suppose a poor devil comes along in the jim-jams, with every inch on him jumpin' an' a look in his eyes like a man bein' murdered an' sent ter hell, an' a whine in his voice like a whipped cur, an' the snakes a-chasing of him; an' he hooks me with his finger ter the far end o' the bar, as if he was goin' ter tell me that the world was ended, an' he hangs over the bar an' chews me lug, an' tries to speak, an' breaks off inter a sort o' low shriek, like a terrified woman, an' he says, 'For Mother o' Christ's sake, giv' me a drink!'

An' what am I to do? I bin there meself. I knows what the horrors is. He mighter blued his cheque at the last shanty. But what am I ter do? I put it ter you. If I let him go he might hang hisself ter the nex' leanin' tree.

What's a drink? Yer might arst, I don't mind a drink or two; but when it comes to half a dozen in a day it mounts up, I can tell yer. Drinks is sixpence here, I have to pay for it, an' pay carriage on it. It's all up ter me in the end. I used sometimes ter think it was lucky I wasn't west o' the sixpenny line, where I'd lose a shillin' on every drink I give away.

An' a straight chap that knows me gets a job to take a flock o' sheep or a mob o' cattle ter the bloomin' Gulf, or South Australia, or somewheers, an' loses one of his horses goin' out ter take charge, an' borrers eight quid from me ter buy another. He'll turn up agen in a year or two an' most likely want ter make me take twenty quid for that eight, an' make everybody about the place blind drunk, but I've got ter wait, an' the wine an' sperit merchants an' the brewery won't. They know I can't do without liquor in the place.

An' lars' rain Jimmy Nowlett, the bullick driver, gets bogged over his axle trees back there on the Blacksoil Plains between two flooded billerbongs, an' prays till the country steams an' his soul's busted, an' his throat like a lime kiln. He taps a keg o' rum or beer ter keep his throat in workin' order. I don't mind that at all, but him an' his mates git floodbound for near a week, an' broach more kegs, an' go on a howlin' spree in ther mud, an' spill mor'n they swipe, an' leave a tarpaulin off a load, an' the flour gets wet, an' the sugar runs out of the bags like syrup, an', what's a feller ter do? Do yer expect me to set the law onter Jimmy? I've knowned him all my life, an' he knowed my father afore I was born. He's been on the roads this forty year till he's as thin as a rat, and as poor as a myall black; an' he's got a family ter keep back there in Bourke. No, I have ter pay for it in the end, an' it all mounts up, I can tell yer.

An' suppose some poor devil of a new chum black sheep comes along, staggerin' from one side of the track to the other, and spoutin' poetry; dyin' o' heat or fever, or heartbreak an' home-sickness, or a life o' disserpation he'd led in England, an' without a sprat on him, an' no claim on the Bush; an' I ketches him in me arms as he stumbles inter the bar, an' he wants me ter hold him up while he turns English inter Greek for me. An' I put him ter bed, an' he gits worse, an' I have ter send the buggy twenty mile for a doctor—an' pay him. An' the jackaroo gits worse, an' has ter be watched an' nursed an' held down sometimes; an' he raves about his home an' mother in England, an' the blarsted university that he was eddicated at, an' a woman, an' somethin' that sounds like poetry in French; an' he upsets my missus a lot, an' makes her blubber. An' he dies, an' I have ter pay a man ter bury him (an' knock up a sort o' fence round the grave arterwards ter keep the stock out), an' send the buggy agen for a parson, an', well, what's a man ter do? I couldn't let him wander away an' die like a dog in the scrub, an' be shoved underground like a dog, too, if his body was ever found. The government might pay ter bury him, but there ain't never been a pauper funeral from my house yet, an' there won't be one if I can help it, except it be meself.

An' then there's the bother goin' through his papers to try an' find out who he was an' where his friends is. An' I have ter get the missus to write a letter to his people, an' we have ter make up lies about how he died ter make it easier for 'em. An' goin' through his letters, the missus comes across a portrait an' a locket of hair, an' letters from his mother an' sisters an' girl; an' they upset her, an' she blubbers agin, an' gits sentimental, like she useter long ago when we was first married.

There was one bit of poetry, I forgit it now, that that there jackaroo kep' sayin' over an' over agen till it buzzed in me head; an', weeks after, I'd ketch the missus metterin' it to herself in the kitchen till I thought she was goin' ratty.

An' we gets a letter from the jackaroo's friends that puts us to a lot more bother. I hate havin' anythin' to do with letters. An' some-one's sure to say he was lambed down an' cleaned out an' poisoned with bad bush liquor at my place. It's almost enough ter make a man wish there *was* a recordin' angel.

An' what's the end of it? I got the blazin' bailiff in the place now! I can't shot him out because he's a decent, hard-up, poor devil from Bourke, with consumption or somethin', an' he's been talking to the missus about his missus an' kids; an' I see no chance of gittin' rid of him, unless the shearers come along with their cheques from West-o'-Sunday nex' week and act straight by me. Like as not I'll have ter roll up me swag an' take the track meself in the end. They say publicans are damned, an' I think so, too; an' I wish I'd bin operated on before ever I seen a pub.

# THE PUBLICAN AT THE PEARLY GATE

**Anonymous**

A publican stood at the Pearly Gate,
His head was bent, and low;
He meekly asked the Man in White
'Which way, mate, do I go?'
'What have you done,' Saint Peter said,
'That you should come up here?'
'I kept a public house below
For many and many a year.'
Saint Peter opened wide the gate
And gently pressed the bell.
'Come right inside and choose a harp—
*You've had your share of hell!*'

# SIX O'CLOCK MADNESS

## Jim Haynes

'Australians have always been enthusiastic, if
not very intelligent, drinkers.'

Sidney J. Baker, 1945

It seemed like a good idea at the time.

Close the pubs at six o'clock, instead of at eleven, and working
men would have time for one or two drinks and then would go
home to be model fathers and husbands.

Or so they thought, in 1916, when they voted to change the law.

The temperance league and various women's groups had been
lobbying for a change in licensing laws for decades. Members of
the Women's Christian Temperance Union were asked to sign a
'Pledge Card' and carry it at all times. The pledge read:

I hereby solemnly promise, God helping me, to abstain from all
distilled, fermented and malt liquors, including wine, beer and
cider, and to employ all proper means to discourage the use of
and traffic in the same.

The temperance movement began in the 1820s and gathered
momentum with the founding of the Salvation Army in 1864.
By the 1870s rallies, marches and meetings commonly called for
various levels of alcohol restriction, from stricter licensing laws

and earlier closing times, to complete prohibition. By the 1890s the movement, as a political force, was making its presence strongly felt in the United Kingdom, United States, Canada, New Zealand and Australia.

Popular slogans of the day, like 'Lips that touch liquor will never touch mine' and 'Girls—wait for a temperance man', encouraged women to marry teetotallers.

The outbreak of war in 1914 gave added impetus to the call for sobriety and restraint. There was a feeling that, while men were dying by the thousands for their nation, we should practise austerity and moral decency at home. Churches and temperance groups called for a reduction in drinking and leisure activities as part of the war effort.

Laws applying to liquor trading were, of course, a state matter and the first state to vote for six o'clock closing was South Australia, at a referendum held in conjunction with a state election on 27 March 1915.

South Australia was originally planned and set up quite differently to the eastern colonies and is the only state in Australia that has no heritage of convict transportation. This has always made South Australia seem subtly socially and culturally 'different' to Australia's other states. State capital Adelaide was known as the 'City of Churches' and, until the 1960s, South Australia had the reputation of being our most conservative state. Outsiders even used the disparaging term 'the wowser state' when referring to South Australia before the 'Dunstan Era' of the 1960s and 1970s changed its reputation.

The temperance movement had been especially active in South Australia from the 1840s, within a decade of the colony's creation. In 1915 the state parliament listened to a deputation from the temperance league and voted to put the question of pub closing time to a referendum. The case put to the parliament mentioned all the wartime arguments and also claimed that crime was alcohol related. The temperance league campaigned for votes for a 6 p.m. closing time with the slogan, 'Lock up the liquor—not the man'.

Voters were given a choice of every hour from six to eleven

o'clock, and 56 per cent voted for 6 p.m. and 34 per cent for 11 p.m. The remaining 10 per cent was spread between the other four options.

And that's how South Australia became the first state to introduce six o'clock closing. It would also be the last state to abandon the idea, 52 years and six months later, on 28 September 1967.

The situation in New South Wales was quite different.

In December 1913 New South Wales voted the Holman Labor Government back into power with a substantial majority after Labor went to the polls with a policy of leaving the pub closing time at 11 p.m. Two and a half years later, in a referendum in June 1916, less than 0.5 per cent of voters chose 11 p.m.

Voters were given the same options as South Australians, a choice of six hours from 6 p.m. to 11 p.m. In New South Wales 63 per cent voted to close pubs at 6 p.m. and 35 per cent voted for 9 p.m.

There is a fairly obvious reason for the turnaround in attitude.

The soldiers' riot of 1916, as described in my story 'The Valentine's Day Mutiny' (see page 83), was an incident that shocked the citizens of Sydney and the rest of New South Wales; although it is subsequently rarely mentioned in any lists of historically important events. The military and the censors tried to push it under the carpet as quickly as possible, but it was widely reported in detail at the time. New South Wales voted on pub closing times almost exactly four months after the event itself, and just three months after accounts of the court cases and court-martial results were published.

The concern generated by this alcohol-fuelled riot produced a vote for 6 p.m. closing that was significantly larger in New South Wales than in the supposedly 'wowser' state of South Australia.

The reason for the strong second choice in New South Wales—about one third voted for 9 p.m.—was that the liquor industry and hoteliers, who were frightened of the groundswell of support for six o'clock closing and the obvious voter backlash from the soldiers' riot, fought a rearguard action and campaigned heavily for a 9 p.m. compromise. It was a lost cause, but 9 p.m. garnered most of the votes that didn't go to the 6 p.m. option.

Victoria and Tasmania followed suit and introduced 6 p.m. closing before the end of 1916, but Western Australia and Queensland held out and never introduced it. Western Australia chose to simply close pubs at 9 p.m. as a wartime measure, and Queensland left things as they were, 11 p.m. closing, until well after the war, but introduced 8 p.m. closing in 1923 and raised the legal drinking age to 21 years.

Once six o'clock closing was 'in' it proved very hard to get it 'out' again after World War I ended. Various states tried to change the law by legislation or another vote, but all attempts to end six o'clock closing failed until after World War II, apart from Tasmania where it ended in 1937.

A move to change the law by legislation, debated in South Australian Parliament in 1938, was met with rallies and protests from women's groups who mobilised in a campaign with the slogan, 'Hands off 6 o'clock closing—Demand a referendum'.

There is a photo showing a group of rather dour matrons holding the signs outside Parliament House on North Terrace. They are a fierce-looking band, all dressed in black. I'm tempted to say their husbands would be the very ones who wanted to stay longer at the pub, but I suspect their husbands never went near pubs—and I'd hate to be accused of reinforcing stereotypes.

Needless to say, the women won the day. There was no change to the law in South Australia until 1967.

By the late 1930s state governments were starting to consider the need to reform licensing laws, but during World War II other priorities made the complex issues involved too difficult to deal with. The war also exacerbated some of the problems and inequities of six o'clock closing. American servicemen stationed in Australia had access to alcohol 'after hours' in their canteens, and officers and politicians dining at nightclubs like Romano's didn't go short of a drink.

While most states reported a short-term decrease in alcohol-related crime after 1916, the negative effects of six o'clock closing in Australia were far-reaching and culturally and socially damaging.

From the very beginning there was a strong sense of class

inequality about working men being denied alcohol while the members of the elite 'gentlemen's clubs' and patrons in expensive nightclubs and restaurants could drink all evening.

On the very first night of six o'clock closing in Adelaide in 1915, there was a noisy demonstration outside the exclusive Adelaide Club in North Adelaide as disgruntled working men, denied a beer, made their feelings known about those who could drink freely in their fortress of privileged superiority. All towns and cities had such clubs for the wealthy and elite.

The new law was to have a profound effect on the nature and development of clubs in several states, but most particularly in New South Wales.

It's a fairly well worn maxim that the best way to make something attractive to criminals is to ban it or restrict it. Organised crime increased rapidly during the era of six o'clock closing. Criminals and potential criminals were gifted an opportunity to establish empires based on what many thought was a 'reasonable' and relatively 'harmless' activity—having a drink after 6 p.m.

As a pretty naive working-class kid growing up in Sydney, even I knew that there were 'sly grog shops' in most suburbs, run by the local neighbourhood operator who was not seen as a 'criminal' any more than the local SP bookie was.

I also knew that 'Thommo's two-up school' and sly grog business operated almost openly with police turning a blind eye. I knew that Kate Leigh and Tilly Devine were 'characters' who provided various services after dark and sometimes caused problems for police, settling their differences by employing the services of razor gangs.

I heard those stories from my mother, a very decent, respectable woman who grew up in Sydney during the time of six o'clock closing and had never been in a pub in her life. She seemed to accept that these things happened as a matter of course and didn't threaten or bother 'normal people' like us very much.

My point here is that silly laws lead to normal, reasonable people accepting a certain level of criminality. And that's what happened during the era of six o'clock closing. Illegal gambling was rife in every suburb of Sydney and liquor was available after hours if you wanted to pay more for it.

Kate Leigh and Tilly Devine were actually dangerous, ruthless women who built criminal empires based on sly grog and prostitution. Kate Leigh was also alleged to import heroin and cocaine.

The natural corollary to accepted levels of crime and well-organised criminal networks is, of course, police corruption. The cost of having six o'clock closing for four decades was police corruption on a massive scale in New South Wales. Certain 'arrangements' were in place between police and 'sly grog' sellers, nightclub owners, brothel keepers and other criminals. This behaviour was deeply ingrained and elements of the corruption survived well into the 1970s, 80s and 90s, leading to many recriminations and royal commissions.

The most far-reaching legacy of six o'clock closing, however, was the effect on our drinking habits and consequently our socialising habits. This was influenced, strange as it may seem, by pub architecture and other factors that led to restrictions on females being allowed in bars. The development of an acceptance of certain types of social behaviour and gender stereotypes within our culture led to some damaging and unhealthy attitudes, which are only now starting to fade into history.

Pub architecture and floor plans quickly changed to accommodate the 'six o'clock swill' and our pubs became what English humourist Willie Rushton described as 'vast tiled puking parlours'.

Rushton was referring to Sydney pubs (in his witty exposé of Aussie life entitled *The I-Didn't-Know-The-Way-To-King's-Cross-When-I-First-Came-Here-But-Look-At-Me-Now Book*). Melbourne social commentator and journalist Keith Dunstan described one of the huge bars in Melbourne as 'a large room, with a cold lavatory-like atmosphere, but filled with pushing men. There are no seats, no tables, no stools, no clutter that might interfere with the high-speed action.'

The 'high-speed action' referred to the use of high-powered 'guns' attached to hoses several metres long, which delivered beer into glasses at what Keith Dunstan called 'a frightening speed'.

Most of the floor space in the pubs was made into one huge tiled room without any furniture, except perhaps for a small shelf running around the walls at head height, just wide enough for a glass. This was so men could buy multiple beers at a time and drink them one after the other. In less fancy pubs, men put their beers between their feet on the floor and stood over them, trying not to move their feet when bumped—it was shoulder to shoulder in those rooms from 5 to 6 p.m.

Bars with fireplaces, card tables and pool tables disappeared—except for one small room where 'ladies' or couples were permitted to sit and drink the same alcohol for a slightly higher price. Called 'the ladies parlour' or 'tap room', these bars had a small window, which opened into the behind-the-bar area in the main bar. Many had a sliding cover so the ladies didn't have to hear the language or see the guzzling in the main bar. A tap on the slide called the barman to open it and serve the drinks then slide it shut. It was illegal for women to enter the main bar of a pub in most states of Australia. The social separation of the sexes was a matter of law.

These small bars were considered a nuisance by some publicans, who became complacent and stopped bothering to provide any 'extras' in their establishments. Many were happy to make 90 per cent of their sales in the hour before serving stopped at 6 p.m. By 6.15 p.m. men had to finish their drinks and be out—and the bars were then hosed out. Spending on furniture or comfort was a waste of time and money.

For decades after six o'clock closing ended, many main bars, or 'front' bars, stayed the same as they had been during the era of the 'swill'. The small 'ladies' bars became the 'saloon bar' where you could sit down to drink and pay a few extra cents for your beer. Most pubs were slowly modernised, in keeping with social changes, in the 1980s and 90s.

The notorious 'six o'clock swill' is often depicted in our art and literature as men drinking flat out for an hour or more on an empty stomach, then staggering home trying not to vomit. One of the placard slogans in a photo of women opposing any change to six o'clock closing reads, 'We want our men at home!' Sadly, that's what many women got, a husband home around 7 p.m. every night—drunk.

All these factors led to a social barrier being placed between men and women. Couples wanting to have a quiet drink together had no way of doing so other than to drink at home 'in front of the children' (which was not considered particularly 'decent' at the time) or by being affluent enough to join a club of some sort.

A man meeting his wife, or any woman, for a drink after work would be relegated to the tap room or parlour, and would have to pay more for the drinks, put up with the noise from the main bar and wait for ages to be served while the demand in the main bar was met. Then he would face the horror of closing time, escorting his female partner out of the pub through the exodus of staggering drunks, often along vomit-splattered footpaths.

While home life was a nightmare for many wives of working men, who only saw their husbands briefly each evening before they passed out drunk, there were some men and women who preferred to have a drink and socialise together in comfort. After World War II, men who had served overseas realised that all-male binge drinking was not a worldwide phenomenon. Having a million American servicemen stationed in Australia, with more sophisticated attitudes towards women and alcohol, was also an eye-opening experience for many women—and even for some Australian men! Returned men started up RSL Clubs, Legion Clubs and Servicemen's Clubs after the war.

In New South Wales the McKell and McGirr Labor governments became worried about alcohol-related crime and the messy licensing laws. In 1947 another referendum was put to voters, this time offering the choices of 6 p.m., 9 p.m. and 10 p.m. Amazingly, 62 per cent of voters chose to keep six o'clock—almost the same percentage that voted that way in 1916—while 36 per cent wanted 10 p.m. and only 2 per cent voted for the compromise of 9 p.m. closing.

Ironically it was mostly women who wanted to keep early closing, perhaps in the mistaken belief that more pub time would mean a longer 'swill', rather than taking away the need for one.

Finally, in June 1951, the McGirr Labor Government established a royal commission into the *Liquor Act* and the way it was being implemented. The commissioner was Justice Maxwell; he held 140 hearings and examined 411 witnesses and more than 100 written submissions over almost three years.

His report was delivered to the Cahill Labor Government in March 1954 and recommended sweeping changes to the *Liquor Act*. Most notably he concluded that:

> There can be no doubt upon the evidence that in the metropolitan area conditions associated with six o'clock closing are deplorable; apart from any other consideration, a refusal to attempt some reform involved, in my opinion, the conscious perpetuation of a clearly established evil; in addition the present closing hour encourages sly grog and after-hour trading at 'Black Market rates'.

Among many other recommendations, Justice Maxwell suggested there were two that were pertinent to the end of 6 p.m. closing and the future of drinking and gambling in New South Wales:

> That the liquor act should be amended to provide for additional club licences on the proviso that licences only be granted to well conducted clubs, which were meeting a genuine need in the community, and not causing unfair competition in their local neighbourhood. He further recommended that there should be priorities in granting of licences, particularly for clubs already in existence, and special provisions be made for R.S.L. clubs within this framework.

So, New South Wales was set on the path to being the leading state for licensed clubs, which established a whole new community lifestyle and helped solve some of the problems associated with the 'six o'clock swill'—while also clearing the way for the plague of poker-machine gambling and gambling-related crime!

The last of the recommendations that concern us from the Maxwell Royal Commission is the one that strongly suggests the government should once again not hesitate in 'seeking the views of the public on the requirement to create longer opening hours for licensed venues'.

In a stand-alone referendum on 13 November 1955, New South Wales voters were given a simple choice—6 p.m. or 10 p.m. closing. The government supported the royal commission findings and hoped for a 10 p.m. vote, but it was a close call.

The final vote was 49.73 per cent for 6 p.m. and 50.27 per cent for 10 p.m. A mere 9792 vote majority in a total of 1,795,272 formal votes! There were 41,794 informal votes, probably due to many not agreeing with either of the time options.

Victoria took another decade to follow suit but no vote was required. Justice Archibald McDonald Fraser, Chairman of the Licensing Board, visited Europe and the United States to look at licensing laws in operation and recommended the extension of opening hours until ten o'clock. He hoped it would end what he called the culture of 'perpendicular drinking' in Australia. His recommendation was signed into state law on 1 February 1966.

There was no vote in South Australia either, and perhaps that was just as well. The Dunstan Labor Government took six months to get the new *Licensing Act* through state parliament. It finally happened in a close vote on 25 September 1967.

Australia has had an alcohol-plagued history from the beginnings of European settlement. Six o'clock closing made things worse by separating the way we drank and socialised strictly along gender lines, and associating alcohol consumption with binge drinking in a degrading, brutish, all-male environment.

The damage done was long-term—crime and police corruption, the social separation of the sexes, a lasting culture of drinking sessions after work and the pervading mentality of 'men around the keg and women in the kitchen'.

Historian Jonathan King commented in 1976 that many Australians 'cannot shake off the mentality of the six o'clock swill', and American brewer Chuck Hahn noted that, when he arrived here in 1981, '"shouts" were still very much the name of the game and the culture of the six o'clock swill remained'.

It is even the reason why tradesmen turn up to work at your house at the inconvenient hour of 6.45 a.m. Tradesmen changed their working hours when 6 p.m. closing came in, as early starts gave them more time at the pub. They have never changed them back.

A few seconds after six o'clock on 28 September 1967, in the bar of the Challa Gardens Hotel in the Adelaide suburb of Croydon, Don Dunstan, ever the showman, raised a glass of beer to toast the end of the 'clearly established evil' of the 'six o'clock swill' in Australia.

The 'swill' was gone, but its legacy lingered on for the rest of the 20th century and it is part of our history forever.

Don's toast to the end of six o'clock closing might well have been, 'It seemed like a good idea . . . at the time.'

# THE OVERFLOW

**Anonymous**

> Sure, the beer I love to taste it, but it breaks me heart to
>     waste it,
> As the careless barman spills it and the bubbles rise like snow.
> And I somehow rather fancy that the barman's name is
>     Clancy,
> And the waste upon the counter is just Clancy's overflow!

# WHERE THE COOLER BARS GROW

## Lennie Lower

'I've never been thrown out of a pub, but I've fallen into quite a few.'

Benny Bellamacina, 2013

I'm only a city boy. Until a short time ago I'd never seen a sheep all in one piece or with its fur on. That's why when people said to me, 'Go west, young man, or east, if you like, but go,' I went.

Truth to tell, I thought it would be safer. I had a shotgun and a rifle, and a bag of flour, and two sealed kerosene tins of fresh water in the luggage van. I thought of taking some coloured beads for the natives, but decided it was too expensive.

I forget now where it was I went. Anyhow, it was full of wheat silos and flies, and there was a horse standing on three legs under a tree. There were no other signs of life except a faint curl of smoke coming from the hotel chimney.

When I walked into the bar there was nobody there, so I walked out the back into the kitchen and there was nobody there. I went out on the verandah and saw a little old man picking burrs off his socks.

'Good-day!' I said.

'Day!' he replied.

'Where's everybody?' I asked.

'Never heard of him. Unless you mean old Smith. He's down by the crick. You're a stranger, aren't you?'

'Just got off the train. Where's the publican?'

'Do you want a drink?'

'Yes.'

'Orright!'

So we went into the bar and had a drink.

'I want to book a room here,' I told him.

'Don't be silly!' he replied. 'Sleep on the verandah with the rest of us if you've got blankets. They're decoratin' the School of Arts with the sheets. You going to the dance?'

'I can't dance!'

'Strike me pink, who wants to? We leave that to the women. There ought to be some good fights at this one. When I was younger there wasn't a man could stand up to me on the dance floor. Here comes somebody now.'

'Day.'

'Day. Don't bring that horse into the bar! Hang it all, you've been told about that before.'

'He's quiet. I broke him in yesterday. Hear about Snowy? Got his arm caught in the circular saw up at the timber mill.'

'That's bad.'

'Too right it is! They've got to get a new saw. Whoa there!'

'Take him out into the kitchen. The flies are worryin' him.'

'Goodo. Pour me out a beer.'

'Pour it out yourself.'

'Go to bed, you old mummified ox!'

'I'll give you a belt in the ear, you red-headed son of a convict!'

'Give it to your uncle. Giddup!'

'One of me best friends,' said the old man, as the horse was led into the kitchen.

'I suppose,' said the red-headed one, returning, 'it'll be all right if he eats that cake on the kitchen table? Won't do him any harm, will it?'

'That's for supper at the dance!'

'Well, I'll go and take it off him. There's a good bit of it left.'

Outside on the verandah voices were heard.

'I wouldn't sell that dog for a thousand pounds.'

'I wouldn't give you two bob for 'im.'

'You never had two bob in your life. You ever seen a sheep dog trial? That dog has won me more prizes at the Show than ten other dogs.

'Why,' the dog's owner continued, 'you could hang up a fly-veil, point out one particular hole in it and that dog could cut a fly out of the bunch and work him through that hole.'

'Good-day!'

'Day!'

'No sign of rain yet.'

'No. I heard tell of a swaggie who had to walk eighty miles to get water to boil his billy, and when he got there he found he'd forgotten his cup and saucer, and by the time he walked back with his cup and saucer there was a bushfire in the water-hole, it was that dry.'

'Don't bring your horses into the bar!'

'Don't take any notice of the old crank. Why don't you put this beer out in the sun to get cool? If it was any flatter you'd have to serve it in a plate. Going to the Show this year?'

'Of course I am. Why don't you teach that horse manners?'

'Good-day, Mrs Smith.'

'Who put that horse in my kitchen?'

'Is he in the kitchen? Well, what do you think of that!'

'Fancy him being in the kitchen!'

'In the kitchen, of all places!'

'Who could have let him in?'

'Never mind about that. Get him out at once, Jack! Wipe up that counter. I told you to cut some wood this morning. And put the dog outside and get the broom and sweep up the bar. Wash those glasses first.'

By this time we were all out on the verandah.

'She hasn't found out about the horse eating the cake yet,' said somebody.

'Better go for a walk somewhere, eh?'

———

But that was all years ago. They've got radios and refrigerators in the bush now, and that's why you see me mournfully wandering about the cattle stalls at Show time. I'm thinking of the good old days before the squatters all took up polo and started knitting their own berets. When men were men and women were useful about the farm when the plough horse took sick.

> Wrap me up in my stockwhip and blanket
> And bury me deep down below
> Where the farm implement salesman won't molest me,
> In the shades where the cooler bars grow.
> Ah, me!

# THE SHANTY BY THE WAY

## Traditional/E.J. Overbury

In the first-rate business section
Where two well-known roads do meet,
Stands a very grand erection,
Welcome rest to weary feet.
If a moment you should linger,
'Tis a case for all that day,
For your cash they'll surely finger
In the shanty by the way.
Rows of bottles standing empty
Labelled with bright blue and gold—
Beer's so cold it needs no icing
From the cellars damp and cold.
Cards and billiards always ready,
Landlord presses us to stay,
How the deuce can man keep sober
In the shanty by the way?
Shoulder up your swag and wander
Thirsty, penniless you'll stray,
For your cash you'll surely squander
In the shanty by the way.

# CHARLIE'S STORY

## Jim Haynes

> 'Work is the curse of the drinking classes.'
>
> Oscar Wilde, c.1885

My father always called me Charlie, though I was christened Leonard. Mum wanted me called Leonard and he wanted me called Edward, after his dad.

Mum didn't want me called Edward; she said, 'I don't want him called Neddy!'

'Well, I don't want him called Leonard,' my father said, 'it sounds like a poofter.'

Dad lost the battle of the names and I was christened Leonard. He never called me Leonard or Len but he didn't call me Edward or Eddie, either, that would have been sour grapes and he wasn't one to hold a grudge, so he called me Charlie.

My dad's real name was Stanley, but he never avoided a fight and tended to settle things with his fists, so he was always called Wacker, or Wack.

He was about five-foot-ten and solid. He weighed around fourteen stone and was a wild bastard when pissed. You had to hold 'em up when you fought him or it was 'one-two . . . under and over' . . . and you were on your arse.

Before the war he worked in a tyre factory, moulding tyres. He'd come home in the afternoon after a shower at work with the rubber still coming out of his skin. He'd have another shower at home, eat dinner and go to bed, same every day . . . dead tired.

He never drank through the week, only on Saturday. Saturday was his day out. Blue pin-striped suit, white silk shirt which Mum had made, red, white and blue tie, shoes highly polished, he'd leave for the football about eleven o'clock in the morning . . . match of the day at the Sydney Cricket Ground.

We lived on a bit of a hill and our street sloped up steeply. About six o'clock most Saturdays he'd make his way up the street, pissed as a parrot. He'd get within a few houses of our place and then he'd sit in the gutter.

After a while he'd start to call out, 'Charlie . . . Charlie . . . come and get me!' His clothes would be crumpled and dirty. Sometimes there'd be a mark or two around one eye where'd he'd been in a blue.

Mum would be all dressed up ready to go dancing. Most Saturdays she and her sister Stella went dancing at the local Palais or maybe even in town, at the Trocadero. It was all very respectable.

I'd go down the hill and get him. As soon as I got him up the few steps and inside the house, he'd take out his mouth organ. His foot would start to go, tap, tap, tap, and he'd sit in the lounge and play the same three tunes over and over: 'Pack Up Your Troubles', 'Click Go the Shears' and 'Red River Valley'.

Pretty much as soon as he came in, Mum was off to go dancing with Stella.

Sometimes he'd want me to see Mrs Kershaw, the SP bookie up the street, to put a few bob each way on the dogs for him.

I'd say, 'Dad, I wanna go to bed. I'm tired, I've been playing football.'

'Did you score any tries?' he'd ask me.

If I told him 'no', he'd say, 'You'll never make a footballer, you're better off being a pug.'

After the war he acted as my second at the only proper fight I ever had in a boxing ring. I fought a draw over six rounds on an undercard at the stadium. All his mates were there and he got more applause for his towel waving between rounds than I got for my boxing.

My dad joined the army when the war started and fought in the Middle East. He was one of the Rats of Tobruk and was pretty badly wounded. When he came home he spent a year in Concord Repat Hospital.

I was seventeen when the war finished and my parents divorced. I visited the hospital but didn't see him much when he got out. He got a job as a cellar-man at a pub in Botany and eventually remarried. He married the publican's sister.

I'd see him now and then for a beer at the pub if I was in the vicinity. Blokes I knew at work or football would sometimes say, 'I saw your dad the other day.'

I'd say, 'Oh, okay. How is he, all right?'

They'd say, 'Yeah he's good,' and that was that.

I had a few different jobs in those few years and when I was nineteen I decided to join the police force.

My dad didn't like coppers, never had, so he stopped talking to me when I joined the police.

If I called into the pub and asked for him, he was always 'busy in the cellar' or 'gone out'.

One day I walked into the pub and he was talking to the barman. They were both behind the bar and I stood there waiting for their conversation to finish.

When they finished talking my dad just turned to me; I knew he'd seen me standing there. He said, 'What do you want?'

I said, 'Nothing, I was just in the neighbourhood.'

He just stood there in his shirt sleeves holding a dirty white cloth in one hand.

'No son of mine should be a copper,' was all he said. So I left.

After that I didn't hear from him for over five years and blokes I knew stopped saying they'd seen my dad.

———

One Sunday morning about six years after I joined the police force, I was on duty with Bill Foster at Redfern Police Station. We got a phone call to say that the old lame billiard marker from the snooker room above the newsagent had copped a dreadful bashing for no real reason. Evidently he was in a bad way.

Billiard markers usually held bets for games played for money in snooker rooms. Gambling was illegal, of course, but it was standard practice. We knew that room was pretty straight. Some of the local thugs had probably tried to stand over him and he'd stood his ground and copped it.

'Got any names?' I asked Bill.

'Donaldson and Sanders . . . they're heading for the railway station.'

'Come on,' I said, 'bring your stick and we'll find the bastards.'

As luck would have it, we ran into them at Redfern Station, between the station entrance and the turnstiles. I said to Bill, 'You take Sanders and I'll take Donaldson.'

Bill got Sanders pretty quick, not much resistance there, but Donaldson and I mixed it for a few until I knocked him down. He looked at me from the ground and said, 'The only way you're taking me anywhere is by the heels.'

'Okay,' I said, 'you're coming by the heels.'

I grabbed him by the heels and dragged him about five or six yards till he said, 'All right, I'll walk.'

We got them down to the station and charged them. The following morning we went to court, got a remand, and that was that, pretty much.

About a week later I got a phone call from my father. He just said, 'I wanna see you.'

I said, 'All right, I finish at three, I'll come up to the pub and see you. What's it about?'

'Never mind,' he said, 'just come and see me.'

I went to see him when my shift finished. I thought I might be in for a smack in the ear so I stood back a bit from him as I said g'day.

'Did you give Donaldson a kicking?' he asked.

'Hey, c'mon,' I said, 'you taught me better than that. I dragged him along by the heels for a few yards but I didn't give him any kicking.'

'What about the other bloke, Sanders?'

'No,' I said, 'he came quietly, he was no problem.'

'Donaldson reckons you gave him a kicking while he was down. He's in the front bar now, let's go and front him.'

'Fine by me,' I said. 'He's telling lies.'

My father looked at me for a long moment, then he asked, 'You sure you're telling me the absolute truth?'

I met his eyes with mine and nodded.

'Right,' he said. 'C'mon.'

When we walked into the front bar Donaldson was on a stool near the street door with a schooner of beer in front of him. He took one look at the two of us together and the colour drained from his face as his brain ticked over, putting two and two together. Then he was off. He just took off like a rocket out the door.

My dad said, 'Never mind, I'll catch up with him one day.'

As we turned to walk back the way we'd come, he asked, matter-of-factly, 'What are you doing Saturday?'

'Nothing,' I said. 'I'm off Saturday.'

'Good,' said my father. 'Meet me here at eleven o'clock . . . we're going to the football.'

# THE GLASS ON THE BAR

Henry Lawson

Three bushmen one morning rode up to an inn,
And one of them called for drinks with a grin;
They'd only returned from a trip to the North,
And, eager to greet them, the landlord came forth,
He absently poured out a glass of Three Star,
And set down that drink with the rest on the bar.
'There, that is for Harry,' he said, 'and it's queer,
'Tis the very same glass that he drank from last year;
His name's on the glass, you can read it like print,
He scratched it himself with an old piece of flint;
I remember his drink—it was always Three Star'—
And the landlord looked out through the door of the bar.
He looked at the horses, and counted but three:
'You were always together—where's Harry?' cried he.
Oh, sadly they looked at the glass as they said,
'You may put it away, for our old mate is dead.'
But one, gazing out o'er the ridges afar,
Said, 'We owe him a shout—leave the glass on the bar.'
They thought of the far-away grave on the plain,
They thought of the comrade who came not again,
They lifted their glasses, and sadly they said:
'We drink to the name of the mate who is dead.'
And the sunlight streamed in, and a light like a star

Seemed to glow in the depth of the glass on the bar.
And still in that shanty a tumbler is seen,
It stands by the clock, ever polished and clean;
And often the strangers will read as they pass
The name of a bushman engraved on the glass;
And though on the shelf but a dozen there are,
That glass never stands with the rest on the bar.

# THE SIX O'CLOCK SWELLS

## Frank Daniel

> 'The great advantage of a hotel is that it's a refuge from home life.'
>
> George Bernard Shaw, 1898

Six o'clock closing at the pubs was supposed to be the law when we were growing up. In our town this law might have existed—but it wasn't really enforced.

When I was a kid women didn't go into pubs—and I didn't know any women who drank beer. As I grew older I discovered a lot of ladies drank beer, but they didn't always let on. Some even smoked cigarettes.

Ladies who drank beer weren't very nice. Neither were ladies who smoked cigarettes. Mother didn't drink beer or smoke cigarettes—and she didn't like other people doing either. However, I don't recall her ever treating them any differently from those who didn't.

As a youngster I had a lot of Aunties and Uncles, most of whom were not even related to our family. The titles were used instead of calling them 'Mister' and 'Missus', just as a mark of more familiar respect.

As I grew older I sorted all this out and gave the family tree a real pruning. I already had enough relations without cultivating any more.

One day around 1951, we met a new 'uncle' and 'aunty', who arrived unexpectedly from Albury on a Friday afternoon.

He was a large bloke with a big belly. He'd known my father during the war and thus, on arrival, was automatically promoted to the rank of 'uncle'. His wife, our new 'aunty', was a thin, quiet lady.

They were towing a thirteen-footer Sunliner caravan behind their 1950 model Ford Custom Sedan. Uncle said his car was a 'Single Spinner'. The bullet-shaped chrome piece in the centre of the grill was apparently known as a 'spinner', and there was only one.

Useful information of course! It would be handy to know stuff like that when we used our expert knowledge of Uncle's Ford to impress our mates.

The car was also a V-eight, and had a 'ton a guts' to tow the plywood caravan 'smack bang round Australia'.

Dad kicked the tyres and tapped his fist on the mudguards and said how solid the car was. He said that we would get one like it one day, 'Soon's we get a few more quid.'

Our car was a Willys Overland. It was a big square old tub. It had lots of room inside, and a rack on the back for carrying luggage. The Willys also had a draw-down blind on the rear window. The Ford didn't have a blind but it had large chrome hub-caps. The Willys had wooden spokes.

My parents showed the visitors around the house and the yard and gave them a look at our modest garden. Mum explained that water was the greatest problem on our farm, and that we had to be very careful as we were down to about two thousand gallons in the tanks.

'It will need to rain soon,' said Dad.

The surprise arrival of our guests caught us low on supplies and Mum asked Dad to run into town and get some things from the shop. It was a rare occurrence, rushing to town like that. Any other time we always managed to 'make do' with whatever could be scraped up.

These visitors must have been very important. They looked as if they were pretty 'well-off'. They didn't look like us. They didn't dress like us. They didn't sound like us.

My older brother, Jim, was much chattier and less shy than me. He soon found out that they didn't know anything about sheep and they didn't even know how to ride a horse.

What sort of people could they be?

Maybe they were what Mum called 'swells', or even 'snobs'.

Dad drove us to town in the Willys—our new Uncle and me and Jim.

We felt that we should have been taken for a drive in the big Ford, but the offer wasn't made, though our visitor made a lot of comments about our old 'faithful', comparing it with his new 'Henry'.

As he talked his big fat arm, outstretched across the back of the front seat, was blocking my view of the speedometer which was in the centre of the dashboard. I liked to keep a good eye on the speedo to see if Dad ever got the old thing over thirty miles per hour, which was about its limit.

Uncle talked a lot about Real Estate and extolled the virtues of 'keeping up with the times' and not letting his cars get too old. Dad looked a bit uncomfortable, but generally seemed to agree with his mate.

The gathering up of the groceries wasn't any great problem. Mr Hogan, the 'General Merchant', was 'pleased to meet' Uncle, who didn't seem terribly pleased to meet Mr Hogan. Uncle kept looking at his watch and at the pub which was just two doors from the store.

With all the goods loaded, Uncle suggested that he and Dad 'should imbibe a little before they ventured home'.

'Uh-oh!' I thought to myself, 'Mum will go crook', especially if imbibing meant drinking beer, which I figured it did.

Then he gave me and Jim a two-bob piece and told us to go and get an ice cream and some lollies at the Milk Bar up the street, while he bought our father a few beers.

Why had we ever had suspicions about this man from Albury? He'd turned out to be a real good bloke. In fact he was a bloody beauty, shouting lollies for us and buying Dad's beer too! Gawd, that would save Dad a heap of dough. He'd soon be able to buy that new Ford that he was interested in.

We didn't realise that buying Dad a few beers meant that Dad had to buy a few more for Uncle. Nor did we realise that if a couple of the locals met Uncle, and then bought him a beer, that meant that Dad and Uncle had to join that 'shout' and drink a few more to square up.

For us kids, the pub was one of the 'Wonders of the World'. Peering through the doorway into that dark mysterious place felt to us like we were encroaching into the secrets of some exotic religious sect. It was a bit like us wondering what it was like inside the Church of England, where the nuns said we were forbidden to ever go.

Drinking beer was a complicated arrangement, accompanied by a continual hubbub of noise and lots of laughter—and it always seemed to last until well after six o'clock.

Hanging around waiting didn't concern us too much on this occasion as Uncle slipped us a few more bob and told us to 'disappear for a little bit longer'. He also advised us 'not to tell the women' that he and Dad had been drinking.

'Blimey!' said Jim, when Uncle went back into the pub, 'we ain't never had more than a shilling at the one time before in our lives.'

He was right too.

When the publican decided that he had overstepped closing time by a sufficiently profitable margin of about two and a half hours, but it was still early enough not to annoy the local Constabulary, he evicted all his patrons from the bar.

We watched the exodus and it was hard to imagine that so many people had been able to fit inside the bar at the same time. They were all laughing and some were wobbling—and one bloke fell over.

Two others tried in vain to help him to his feet and finally Dad came to their assistance and helped get the bloke up.

Evidently they were shearers from one of the sheds down near the Lake having a 'cut-out'. As they staggered away Dad commented that some blokes didn't know when they'd had enough.

The trip home in the faithful Willys was memorable—and at times a little scary. We were pleased to see that Dad was not really 'that drunk' after all. He must have been okay because he managed to bring the car back onto the roadway without any trouble on more than three occasions. Jim kept turning to see if the guide posts were still in place as we went along.

Big fat Uncle was sitting quietly in the front with his left elbow out the window, but every now and then he'd suddenly make a comment.

'Hang on to her there, mate!' he said, as Dad battled with the Willys on a bend at about twenty miles an hour.

'She'll be right, mate,' said Dad, 'the old girl knows the way home on her own.'

'Bore it up 'er!' burped Uncle.

He wasn't sounding too much like a swell now. He was as red as beetroot and he kept doing little hiccups which puffed his cheeks out and made his lips pout and give a little hiss each time he exhaled. His face looked fat and round as if he had a mouthful of something and he had three chins now, instead of the two he'd had when he arrived. At times, in the intervals between hiccups, he looked like he was about to explode and, sure enough, about halfway home he let go a huge fart that made the car stink.

That gave me and Jim the giggles, which gradually got out of control. Finally our hysterical giggling roused Dad, who tried to give us a clout by swinging his arm at us over the back of the front seat.

We were pretty safe in the Willys as the rear seat was too far back for him to reach us, but his attempt to discipline us caused the car to leave the main part of the gravel road for a while, before finding its way back to where the grader had been and the road was smooth.

After that we'd snort and start giggling again whenever one of us looked at Uncle. What a funny fat old geezer he seemed to be now.

When we reached our place there was a fight over who would open the front gate. Jim was first out and away and then Uncle decided that he had to get out too, to 'shake hands with his best mate'.

I thought that meant that he'd developed a sudden affection for Jim and wanted to show his respect for him volunteering to open the gate by giving him a manly handshake.

Once he got out, though, he seemed more intent on something else.

He had a pee on the gatepost and while he was busy doing that it must have slipped his mind to shake hands with Jim.

Back at the house Mum and Aunty had managed to gather some bits and pieces together for a meal and only needed a few essentials from the grocery box after all. Some mention of our late arrival was made, but we didn't dob about the men going to the pub.

Dad and Uncle stood outside in the dark, talking and laughing for some time until they were called for tea. Of course they tried to look sober and make out that they hadn't been drinking.

The light from the kerosene lamp in the centre of the table seemed to give Uncle and Dad a kind of rosy glow. Aunty's face had a serious look and her steely eyes were fixed on Uncle. His eyes, on the other hand, were a bit watery and glistened in the flickering glow of the lamp, and he still hiccuped quietly now and then as he ate.

Mum was busy making sure that everybody had enough to eat but Jim and I were not hungry for some strange reason. We'd eaten about four bob's worth of ice cream and chocolate and still had pockets full of lollies.

Then Uncle hiccuped loudly and we started giggling again. Mum went crook on us but Dad said nothing, for fear that his speech might betray his drinking, I suppose.

We had almost controlled our giggles when Uncle reached for a slice of bread and let out another loud fart.

All hell broke loose.

We just couldn't contain ourselves. In an uncontrollable fit of hysterical giggling, Jim slipped off his chair and disappeared under the table. The last we saw of him were his two hands holding a knife and fork, which clawed the tablecloth in an endeavour to slow him down.

Dad did his block. 'Shut-up and eat ya tea!' he roared through a mouthful of meat, peas and potato.

Dad gave Jim a kick under the table which brought him to the surface smartly. In the process he cracked his head on the edge of the table.

Now, Jim had finally put a slice of mutton in his mouth where there was already a well-sucked boiled lolly just before Uncle farted.

When he hit his head he let out a yelp and then started to choke. Before anyone could do anything to help he coughed out the mutton and the lolly and made a bolt for the back door.

The screen door from our kitchen to the back verandah was abused so many times in emergencies like that. Once again it was flung wide open beyond the manufacturer's wildest expectations and then slammed shut.

The mood changed very quickly. Suddenly things didn't seem that funny anymore.

Jim went to sit on the paling fence behind the shearer's hut, which was a good defensive vantage point. Should an attack come from the house yard he could drop down into the orchard and make for the tank-stand behind the laundry. An attack from the rear could be countered by a quick drop into the house yard, where a number of escape routes were available. The safest hiding place of all was under our beds, should access be available through a vacant house.

By the time the meal was over it was way past our bedtime. We had a wash outside by the laundry in an enamel basin, which sat on a large chopping block.

Cold water and Sunlight soap soon put a shine on my face again, and about then Jim decided that it was all clear to return to the ranks.

Some vestige of the earlier hilarity returned when we got to bed. We giggled in whispers until Mum came in and said, 'Quieten down and go to sleep now and you can have another talk to Uncle in the morning.'

But our visitors had a very early breakfast and left straight after.

We never saw them again, ever.

Dad, it seemed, had been convinced about the virtues of keeping up with the times and bought a new car from Heats Motors in Goulburn a few weeks later.

He didn't buy a Ford.

Our new car was a Standard Vanguard.

# THE PRECIOUS WORD

## C.J. Dennis ('Den')

He staggered from the bar-room door,
 A mound of insobriety;
His left leg seeking to ignore
 It's fellow-leg's society.
'Ah,' sniffed a dame across the way,
 With virginal acidity,
'A nice example, I must say,
 To judge by 'is awkwidity.'
He swayed beside the pavement's rim,
 And glared with great ferocity,
While fierce invective poured from him
 In billows of verbosity.
'Ah,' said the dame,
'Just 'ear 'im rave;
 'E's busting with loquacity,
The beer 'as made 'im very brave.
 Jist 'ark at 'is **pubnacity!**'

# THE DAY THE PUB DIDN'T BURN DOWN

## Jim Haynes

> 'All manner of people frequent all manner of public houses.'
>
> Patrick Hamilton, 1930

The palm trees in the courtyard were the cause of all the trouble. The new publican at the Royal reckoned they were 'a bit of an eyesore'. They towered way above the galvanised iron roof and their thick grey trunks took up most of the room in the little courtyard bounded by the bar at the front, the wash-house and store along the sides and the guests' rooms along the back.

The ornamental berries and fronds used to shed regularly onto the pub roof and Old Jimmy the pub handyman reckoned he was 'Getting too old to be forever climbing up on the bloody roof.'

Win Jenkins, who did the cleaning and laundry at the Royal, agreed with him. She was sick of the mess around the courtyard floor causing her a lot of extra work and she voiced that opinion to anyone who would listen. Indeed she spent a lot more time voicing the opinion than she did actually cleaning up the mess in the courtyard.

There wasn't that much cleaning done at the Royal, to be honest. Being the town's 'other pub' meant that a high standard of cleanliness was not really expected. There wasn't much laundry because people only stayed there by mistake, and usually only once. Mopping out the front bar and hosing down the verandah were the main cleaning tasks, or when the pub lived up to its repu- tation of being 'the bloodhouse' and fights erupted, the routine changed to hosing out the front bar as well, rather than persever- ing with a mop.

Nevertheless, Win was of the opinion that 'those bloody old palm trees' made her life a lot harder, and she joined with Jimmy in telling the new publican that the pub would be better off without them.

The new publican listened and nodded.

The trees might still have been safe if Jimmy and Win had been the only voices speaking out against them. After all, Jimmy and Win had said the same thing to a succession of new publicans.

But this time there were other reasons why the trees were threatened.

The first of these was that Dot, the barmaid at the Royal, had also decided the trees were a 'bloody nuisance'.

This was a new development. As a rule Dot didn't bother herself with the territory beyond the bar at the Royal, she didn't need to. Dot ruled the Royal with a fist of iron from the front bar. She didn't need to visit the courtyard or the laundry as long as she controlled the front bar of the Royal.

Dot was a legend in Weelabarabak. Her standard greeting, 'Waddya want?', actually set the standard for small town hospi- tality for miles around. She could prevent a brawl with one word from twenty paces and she possessed an icy stare that could make a drunken shearer think twice about causing trouble.

Nobody really knew why Dot suddenly took an interest in the palm trees. I reckon she just got sick of Win and Jimmy whingeing and decided to resolve the matter by agreeing with them. Whatever the reason, she added her considerable weight to the decision by telling the new publican he should 'get rid of the bloody things'.

This onslaught on the new publican occurred very soon after his arrival at the Royal. The staff knew you didn't have much time to initiate change before a new publican sank into the same state of apathy as all his predecessors and did pretty much nothing except let Dot run the pub from the front bar. So the plot against the palm trees was hatched during his first week in the place.

Even then it might not have succeeded except for one other thing. The new publican had just come from managing a series of pubs that had all been destroyed by fire. He was not quite stupid enough to believe that these fires had been complete accidents, as on at least one occasion he had been told to be away from the premises at a specified time. He was also well aware that the actual owners of these establishments had benefited rather nicely from the demise of each pub by moving the licence to a more heavily populated town.

These experiences had left him wary of sudden fires in the night. He hadn't *always* been told to be away from the premises on relevant dates it seems, and he had consequently become a bit jumpy about the prospect of sudden fires.

So the new publican, perhaps in light of the staff conspiracy against the palm trees—or perhaps solely for reasons of his own—decided firstly that the palm trees *were* a fire hazard and decided secondly to solve this problem in a unique way.

He decided to burn them down.

Well, they were too tall to cut down; they would have caused quite a lot of damage when they fell onto the roof. And that's where they would have fallen because the courtyard was so small.

They would have fallen on the bar, the store, the laundry or the guests' rooms, causing who knew how much damage.

The new publican no doubt thought the palm trees would burn in a quite orderly manner, disintegrating into a fairly neat pile of coal and ash within the courtyard.

He set fire to them quite early one morning, expecting the whole thing to be over and cleaned up by lunchtime. He soaked the trunks with kero and piled some kindling and stove wood around each base and up the fire went, racing on kero fumes into the foliage at the top of each tree.

An excited mob of kids and grown-ups assembled from nowhere to enjoy that strange communal thrill humans always seem to experience in the presence of a really destructive fire.

We were on our way to school as the fire took off, and quickly diverted from our normal course down the side street next to the pub to watch the proceedings, wheeling our bikes as close as we dared so we could see the whole scene inside the courtyard.

The fronds and greenery at the top of the trees burned away very quickly. In a quite spectacular display, the burning vegetation fell to earth in and around the courtyard and on the galvanised iron roof, where it quickly burnt out, leaving a mess of ash to be cleaned up later on by Win and Jimmy.

We 'oohed' and 'arrghed' in time to the bursts of flame and the descent of the largest pieces of burning vegetation, and tried to ignore the adults who told us to 'look out' and 'get off to bloody school and out of the way'.

After that the fire settled down and became rather boring. The thick spongy trunks burned away slowly, apparently from the inside.

As they smouldered the trunks turned blacker and blacker, and a steady column of grey smoke arose from each one and drifted lazily into the clear sky above the courtyard of the Royal Hotel. They looked like two industrial chimneys transplanted into a rural pub courtyard.

After the early spectacle of the blazing vegetation and fiery falling fronds, this was rather mundane to watch and soon the group of onlookers had completely disintegrated, we reluctantly headed to school and the town went about its business.

By lunchtime the new publican had discovered that burning palm trees smoulder for an amazingly long time. So long did they smoulder, in fact, that they had practically been forgotten when the wind strengthened out of the west at about three o'clock that afternoon, just about the same time that the trees really began to disintegrate and fall apart.

The tree trunks had now become two teetering columns of glowing coals and, as the wind picked up, they began raining red-hot embers and quite sizeable lumps of fire all over the pub and its surroundings.

As the hot wind gusted out of a still-clear sky, the scene began to resemble something in a medieval painting of Judgment Day or one of those particularly lurid Old Testament illustrations we were shown in Sunday school—the ones where Egypt suffered plagues and torments because Pharaoh wouldn't let the Israelites go.

These falling embers were far more substantial than the morning shower of burning fronds. The coals continued to burn with substantial intensity upon hitting the ground, the roof, the dry grass around the pub, or the wooden verandahs and walkways inside the courtyard and along the main street in front of the pub.

In fact, by three-twenty, when Mrs Thompson was telling us to tidy up our desks and make sure we'd written our homework into our homework books, the Royal Hotel was in mortal danger of transforming itself from the town's 'other pub' into the town's 'ex-pub'.

The new publican and the few staff who were on duty, along with the few desperate afternoon drinkers, had been stirred into action. Some were filling buckets from the cement tubs in the wash-house and others had been despatched to get help from nearby businesses and dwellings and warn the residents of the possible danger.

In the midst of the growing hysteria Dot the barmaid arrived to start her normal shift. She took one look at the scene, lifted the phone and told the postmaster to call out the Weelabarabak Fire Brigade.

Luckily this was back in the days when the postmaster kept a key to the fire shed, whether he was fire captain or not, so the post-master closed the post office and, along with his postal clerk and a couple of farmers who happened to be collecting mail at the time, hastened to the nearby fire shed, opened the door and, by doing so, magically transformed himself, his postal clerk and the farmers into the adumbral phase of the Weelabarabak Fire Brigade.

The Weelabarabak fire shed contained the fire trailer, which held the brigade's water tank, pump and hose. The Weelabarabak Fire Brigade did not possess a vehicle. In order to get the fire-fighting equipment to the actual fire, the trailer had to be attached to the towbar of the nearest vehicle that possessed a towbar and could be commandeered for the purpose.

As the small group of firemen entered the shed, however, the postal clerk, the brightest of the group, made the observation that the Royal was actually *downhill* from the fire shed and, if they filled the water tank *after* they arrived at the scene of the alleged fire rather than before they left the fire shed, the trailer would be light enough for them to push it to the Royal rather than waste time looking for a vehicle with a towbar. They could then fill the tank from the water mains at the pub and use the pump to direct the water with the necessary force onto the fire.

Gil Stafford had closed his produce store and dashed across the road to become part of the Weelabarabak Fire Brigade while the original group was opening the fire shed. It was Gil who made the suggestion at this point that perhaps the water mains could be connected directly to the brigade pump, thus making the water tank redundant.

Encouraged by the general response that 'it sounded like a good idea', Gil grabbed the length of hose designed to siphon water from rivers and dams into the pump and dashed back to his store to see if he had suitable fittings for its other end.

Meanwhile, the remainder of the Weelabarabak Fire Brigade (a remainder which was growing larger by the minute as local businesses closed and able-bodied men arrived) wheeled the trailer out of the fire shed and began pushing it in the direction of the endangered Royal Hotel. They left the water tank on board for two reasons; one was 'just in case' and the other was that it would take too long to get off. Those who couldn't find a space to help push gathered up sundry items from the fire shed—shovels, buckets and axes—and ran behind, beside or in front of the trailer.

The arrival of this enthusiastic caravan outside the Royal Hotel coincided with the entire student body from Weelabarabak Public School arriving from the opposite direction.

The coming together of these two groups—one made up of kids yelling rather obvious news of fires and fire brigades to each other, and the other consisting of a trailer on which everything rattled, bouncing along at terrifying speed, accompanied by a dozen or fifteen men thumping along in work boots and yelling at us to 'look out'—is certainly the noisiest memory I have of my childhood. But the visual memories I have of that scene, and what happened next, are even better.

In the midst of the confusion Gil Stafford had arrived with an armful of fittings and located the water mains under the pub verandah. Stilsons were applied to the appropriate connections and, with a minimum of fuss and water wastage, the mains were connected to the pump.

Parts of the pub had now started to burn rather seriously and, of course, the remains of the trees themselves were now glowing chimneys of chaos and destruction.

The short hose from the mains had been connected to the intake at the back of the pump and now the fire hose was rolled out and connected to the front of the pump. The pump was started after a few good pulls on the rotor and it sprang into deafening life with a roar and a billow of smoke much blacker than that now arising from various parts of the pub. The hose unwound up the steps, across the verandah, in the front door of the bar and out through the back door into the courtyard like a vengeful canvas python.

The men of the Weelabarabak Fire Brigade positioned them-selves at intervals every few yards or so along the length of the fire hose. They were ready to take the strain like a tug-o'-war team, ready to control the deadly force of water about to be unleashed against the flames which threatened the Royal Hotel.

Us kids were told to 'stand well back' and the word was given to turn the valve and let the pump do its work.

Nobody could remember when the hose had last been checked. It was a rule of the Weelabarabak Fire Brigade that 'in the case of *no fire*' the hose should be checked annually. In other words, if the hose was not used for twelve months, there being no fires in that time, it should be checked to see that it was still in an operational condition.

The problem was that blokes got busy through the year and fire drill wasn't always as regular as it should be. Besides, no one really made a note of whether or not the hose had been used when the brigade was called out and there wasn't always time for a working bee between fires, even if the time between fires stretched into years.

Evidently the hose, made of some kind of rubberised compound covered in canvas, had not been checked for quite a while. The resulting attempt at fire-fighting was spectacular. I can still see it now after all these years.

The water hit the first kink in the hose, where it turned an angle of twenty degrees or so from the trailer to the pub steps, and a jet of water shot out of the hose, soaked the postmaster and arced some fifteen feet into the air. A few yards further down the hose, another stream of water shot out all over the postal clerk, then another stream broke out just under the verandah roof. It went straight up, hit the galvanised iron ceiling and cascaded down over all those on the verandah.

Just at the door of the pub, a double stream shot out laterally, hitting both sides of the door frame. Inside the bar jets continued to spout, at the floor, the wall and the ceiling. Each new spout was just as unexpected as the first and left men jumping and swearing along the length of the hose. It was as if the flow of water was accompanied by some weird electric current.

What we couldn't see from our position outside the pub was that each new eruption of water from the hose was measurably weaker than the last. The funniest scene of all, according to Old Nugget who was inside and told me and Dad later, through tears of laughter, involved the two burliest farmers, who stood braced in the doorway from the bar to the courtyard with the hose nozzle directed at the worst of the fire.

As the jets of water breaking from the hose became weaker and weaker, the two men stood steadfast and resolute, waiting to give the force of water its final direction. But when the stream did reach them, it was not a fearsome pub-saving gush of white water which could be directed into the depths of the ravening fire. It was, in Nugget's own words, 'a woeful little piddle of water which dribbled out the nozzle of the hose and splashed around the farmers' boots'.

While chaos reigned in the bar and on the verandah, and a forlorn puddle formed at the fire-fighting farmers' feet, the fire raged on in the courtyard, totally unaffected by the large amount of misdirected human energy being expended in futile attempts to extinguish it.

Many theories regarding possible remedies for the situation abounded among the men of the Weelabarabak Fire Brigade, most of whom were soaked to the skin. Before the fearless fire-fighters had formulated a really useful Plan B, however, Dot had organised a bucket brigade from the wash-house.

The fires in the courtyard, in the grass around the pub and in various other places, were quickly put out. The soaked fire-fighters joined in meekly, doing exactly as Dot told them until all was under control.

The palm trees were replaced on one side of the courtyard by a half-hearted barbecue and on the other side by a new rotary clothesline. This was meant to make Win's life a bit easier, although she whinged a fair bit that it wouldn't keep still when you were pegging stuff on it.

Locals reckon that's the cleanest the bar of the Royal has ever been, before or since.

# THE OLD 'WHITE HORSE'

## C.J. Dennis ('Den')

(Written in 1933 when the old White Horse Hotel, from
1853 the first changing place for Cobb & Co. coaches on
the Lilydale run, was to be torn down to make way for
brick houses.)

In olden days the old White Horse
  Stood brave against the sky;
And ne'er a teamster shaped his course
  To pass the good inn by.
Far shone its lights o' winter nights
  To beckon weary men;
By the long road where calm life flowed
  It loomed a landmark then.

And many a right good yarn was spun
  Mid pewter-pots agleam;
And many a friendship here begun
  Grew riper as the team
Drew down the road its precious load
  Of merchandise or mail,
And faced the ills of long, steep hills
  To far-off Lilydale.

The tap room rang to many a song,
 While patient teams stood there;
And talk and laughter loud and long
 Held nothing of despair;
For spoke they then, those bearded men,
 Of fortunes shining near—
Spoke with a grand faith in their land,
 A faith that laughed at fear.

Gone are the days and gone the ways
 Of easy, calm content;
Yet few supposed an epoch closed
 The day the old inn went.
Now, past brick homes trim and cold,
 The swift cars, speeding by,
Shall see no beacon as of old,
Shall see no brave White Horse stand bold
 Against a hopeful sky.

# SECTION FOUR
# HANGOVERS

# THE MORNING AFTER

## Col Wilson ('Blue the Shearer')

To-day's the first day of the rest of my life,
And I wish I were dead, but I won't tell the wife.
When I woke up this morning she looked in my eye,
And said: 'How do you feel?' I said: 'Marvellous. Why?'
She told me: 'Last night, my wife's intuition,
Felt some concern for your general condition.'
And then it came back. Last night we had guests,
And I'd entertained with considerable zest.
Still. I wouldn't let on that I wasn't too good,
And I went to the bathroom, as all poets should.
I looked in the mirror, and what did I see?
I was shaving a stranger. That couldn't be me.
I knew I felt crook, but that bloke looked like death,
About to expire on his terminal breath.
But reason prevailed. I accepted my fate,
But how did I get in this terrible state.
It wasn't the sherry. I only had two,
And of whisky and vodka—not more than a few.
Three or four cans of convivial beer.
That can't be the reason I'm feeling so queer.
During dinner, the wines, the white and the red,
But never so much as to go to my head.
Maybe the brandy. But I only had one,

221

And that wasn't enough to have brought me undone.
Now, let's take it slowly. I've just had a thought.
With the coffee and chocolates, I did have some port.
In fact in that company, the port flowed quite well.
So it's due to the port, that I'm feeling like hell.
I know I'll recover. The question is 'When?'
And IF I recover, will it happen again?
In the meantime, I'll try to pretend I'm OK
And hope to survive 'til the end of the day.
And my darling persists with that 'serves you right' smirk.
Whistling away as she does the housework.
I'm damn sure she knows how it cuts like a knife,
'Please God. Can't I swap for a taciturn wife?
I promise I'll never drink port while I live,'
And that is a promise I'll cheerfully give.
I'll just stick to sherry, and whisky and beer,
And white and red wine, and a brandy to clear
All the cobwebs away from my suffering brain,
And port shall not touch my gullet again.
But, I've just thought of something. I think I should wait.
It may NOT be the drink, but something I ate.
I DID have the dips, cheeses, entrees, main meal,
Dessert and some chocolates. No wonder I feel
As though forces of evil are loose in my head,
And my stomach is asking to be put to bed.
And I'm blaming the port, that innocent wine,
Maybe I will have the odd sip again.
In the meantime, my body's in terrible strife—
To-day's the worst day in the rest of my life.

# THE DRUNKEN KANGAROO

Kenneth Cook

> 'Tis not the drinking that is to be blamed, but
> the excess.'
>
> John Selden, (1584–1654)

My deep fear of all Australian animals probably stems from my childhood association with an alcoholic kangaroo.

My father was a policeman and for a time was stationed at Walgett in northern New South Wales. He, my mother and I found ourselves living next door to an old man who kept as a pet a huge red kangaroo.

The old man's name was Benny and he called his kangaroo Les after a famous boxer. Benny was a fuzzy-haired, sparrow-like man with a sweet disposition. Les was almost two metres of muscle and malice. I never saw why Benny was so fond of him.

Les lived in Benny's backyard. It was surrounded by a tall paling fence which he simply hopped over when he wanted to get out. He wanted to get out at least six times a day, and poor old Benny spent most of his life trying to persuade Les to come home. Benny used to get badly bruised in these encounters because the roo had a habit of hitting him with his forepaws, kicking him with his hind legs or whacking him with his tail when Benny tried to catch him.

Sometimes Benny tried to take Les for walks on a lead, and it was a sad sight to see that nice man being dragged through the main street of Walgett by a massive marsupial given to punching, kicking or whacking him with great frequency.

People often advised Benny to turn Les loose, or, better still, to convert him into dog's meat, but Benny would protest that he loved the animal and, contrary to all the evidence, the animal loved him.

At that stage, Les was no problem to anybody else in Walgett and if Benny wanted to maintain an unusual association with a kangaroo, that was his business. Nobody interfered.

My father and I became quite friendly with Benny and often used to help him catch Les and bring him home. It was an exciting business, and I used to enjoy it, particularly as Les never punched, kicked or whacked anybody but Benny.

But then Les took to drink and became a public menace.

There was a brewery in Walgett in those days, and every Wednesday the hops mash was strained off the brew and dumped at the rear of the premises in a large pond.

Les discovered this on one of his jaunts, tasted it and found he loved the beery, sloppy mess. He ate and ate until he fell down in an alcoholic stupor.

Benny learned of this when a messenger from the brewery called to tell him that his bloody kangaroo had dropped dead in the rear of the brewery premises and would he please get the corpse out of there immediately.

Poor old Benny was distraught, and enlisted my father and me to help him. The three of us trooped down to the brewery and found Les not dead, but very, very unconscious.

'He's mortal bad,' keened Benny in his squeaky old voice.

'No, he's not,' said my father, eyeing the great pool of hops mash and noting that the same stuff was liberally splattered over the kangaroo's brutish face. 'He's rotten drunk.'

Benny pleaded with us to help get Les home.

My father was a big man, and strong, and I wasn't bad for my age. Benny wasn't much use. The three of us grabbed Les by the tail and tried to drag him home. But half a ton of comatose kangaroo is hard to drag and we finally had to go and get a draughthorse to do the job. We rolled Les onto a gate and the draughthorse dragged him the half kilometre or so to Benny's backyard.

We left Benny covering Les with a blanket and pressing wet towels to his forehead, if kangaroos can be said to have foreheads.

I was there the next morning when Les finally woke up. Benny was squatting next to him, holding his right paw, as he had apparently been doing all night. Les opened one eye with extreme care. It was very bloodshot. He shut it quickly. There was a long pause, during which Benny clucked and tutted sympathetically, and then the kangaroo opened both bloodshot eyes. I swear he winced.

My memory may be playing me false, but I am convinced that at this point Les very slowly and clumsily scrambled to his feet and leaned against the paling fence, holding both front paws to his head. He groaned.

Kangaroos do groan.

Benny went rushing off to get a bucket of water and Les drank the lot without pausing for breath, which is normally a very difficult thing for a kangaroo to do.

The water seemed to help him a lot. He stood looking reflectively into the empty bucket. Then suddenly he leaped straight over the paling fence and went bolting down the street towards the brewery.

'After him!' squeaked Benny. He flung open the gate and went hobbling after the kangaroo as fast as a man of eighty or so can hobble, which is not very fast.

I ran ahead of him and managed to keep Les in sight. He made straight for the brewery, leaped the two-strand wire fence around the rear of the building, flung himself into the hops mash and began sucking the stuff up as though his life depended on it. He probably felt that it did.

I stood helplessly at the edge of the pond, watching the huge kangaroo, waist-deep in hops mash, plunging his head again and again into the yeasty mess, eating, imbibing, inhaling the whole highly alcoholic mixture. I later realised that I was witnessing a classic case of instant alcoholic addiction.

Benny came panting up and nearly burst into tears when he saw what was happening.

'Come out of it, Les, you naughty kangaroo,' he cried, 'you'll make yourself sick as a dog.'

Les took no notice whatsoever.

'Go and get your father, boy,' squeaked Benny. I shot back home and told my father what was happening. A kindly man, he stroked his beard and thought for a moment.

'He's actually in the pond this time?'

'Yes.'

'So if he takes in enough of the stuff, he'll probably pass out and drown?'

'Yes, I suppose so.'

'Might be the best possible solution,' said my father.

But I was young and fond of Benny. I pleaded with my father to come to the rescue. He eventually collected a rope and the draughthorse and we returned to the brewery.

Quite a crowd had gathered by then. Old Benny was literally in tears as he pleaded with Les to pull himself together and give up the drink. Les determinedly continued to try and absorb enough of the hops mash to render himself insensible.

My father made a lasso out of the rope, threw it over Les's chest and tied the other end around the neck of the draughthorse. Les was hauled from the pond, kicking and grunting and desperately trying to swallow a few more mouthfuls.

As soon as he was on dry land, dripping hops mash, he turned ugly.

This was no comatose, alcohol-sodden marsupial: this was a fighting drunk kangaroo. He leaped at my father, grunting angrily, and knocked him down with one mighty kick. Then he turned on the crowd, who ran away shrieking. Les went after them but was brought up short by the rope around his chest. He turned and went for the draughthorse. The draughthorse looked at him sourly and kicked him in the stomach. Les stood for a moment, gasping, and Benny rushed in and threw his arms around the beast. Les drew back his left paw, struck and knocked Benny flat on his back.

My father had recovered a little by then but was still obviously dazed. He drew his revolver and advanced on Les, shouting, 'Surrender in the name of the king!'

Les just stood there, grunting furiously.

'Surrender in the king's name,' repeated my father, pointing his revolver, 'or I'll blow your bloody head off!'

Benny was on his feet now and he flung himself between my father and Les. The conversation became inconsequential.

'You can't shoot a kangaroo,' said Benny.

'Yes, I can,' said my father. 'I have, often.'

'But this is a civilised kangaroo,' said Benny. 'You can't shoot a civilised kangaroo without a charge.'

'The charge is being drunk and disorderly,' roared my father.

'But you don't shoot people for being drunk and disorderly,' pleaded Benny.

'Kangaroos aren't people,' said my father, who could never resist an argument.

'There you are,' said Benny triumphantly. 'That's exactly what I mean.'

'Eh?' said my father.

Les, meanwhile, on a slack rope, had slipped back into the pond and was absorbing hops mash again.

'You wouldn't shoot my old mate, would you, man?' asked Benny piteously.

My father, whose head seemed to be clearing, began to see the funny side of the situation. He slipped his revolver back into its holster.

'All right,' he said, 'I'll tell you what we'll do. Let him guzzle on for a while. He'll get dopey, then we'll drag him out and toss him in the lock-up until he's sober.'

So that's what we did. Les went on tucking into the hops for about half an hour, then he started to sway, went cross-eyed and was about to collapse when my father began to lead away the draughthorse, to which Les was still attached.

'What are you doing with my kangaroo?' squeaked Benny.

'I told you,' said my father. 'I'm going to gaol him until he sobers up.'

He pulled out his handcuffs, preparatory to handcuffing Les's legs together, if you can handcuff legs.

'How long are you going to lock him up for?' asked Benny.

'Until I'm satisfied that he's no longer a public danger,' said my father.

'But you can't do that without charging him,' said Benny. 'I'll have habeas corpus on you.'

'Then I'll charge him,' said my father desperately.

'With what?'

'Disturbing the peace, being drunk and disorderly, assault, resisting arrest, causing a public disturbance. I've got enough on your bloody kangaroo to keep him in gaol for life. Now stop making a fuss, or I'll shoot him dead for trying to escape.'

'But he's not trying to escape,' said Benny plaintively.

'What's that got to do with it?' asked my father.

'I'm going to get a lawyer,' cried Benny and hobbled away purposefully.

While all this legal argument was going on, Les unobtrusively slipped out of the noose and went bounding drunkenly up the main street. He was far from being comatose; he was in an advanced state of delirium tremens.

The street was packed with horses and sulkies, drays, motor cars, shoppers, old ladies and small children.

Les was bounding higher and more wildly than any sober kangaroo possibly could. Emitting loud explosive grunts, he went over the head of a horse harnessed to a cart and kicked it on the nose as he passed. The horse whinnied, reared and bolted. Les blundered into a shop window and smashed it. Two old ladies had hysterics.

My father, revolver drawn again, went racing after the kangaroo, but his shooting was restricted by fear of killing too many innocent civilians. Les stunned an old gentleman with his tail, then did shocking damage to an expensive motor car with his rear claws.

My father got close enough for a safe shot, but missed (he was a rotten marksman) and blew out another shop window. Les leaped over four fat, middle-aged ladies, three of whom fainted. My father tripped over one of them and accidentally shot the tyre of a motor bus. All the passengers started to scream. The main street of Walgett, for the first and probably last time, was like a Marx Bros movie.

Finally Les stopped in front of a pub, as though instinctively looking for more drink. My father caught up with him and loosed off four shots at point-blank range. They all missed and the pub window suffered irreparable damage. But Les's booze-soaked mind finally grasped the fact that he was in real danger. He turned and bolted out of town.

My father commandeered a car and went after him, still shooting, but soon lost him when Les turned off the road and went into the scrub.

Benny was disconsolate. 'I loved that kangaroo,' he told my father reproachfully, 'and now you've frightened him right out of my life.'

Privately my father thought he had done Benny a favour, but he was a soft-hearted policeman and he caught a young wallaby and gave it to the old man as a pet. 'But for God's sake, keep it off the grog,' he warned.

'Well, thank you,' said Benny, wrapping his arms around the wallaby, 'but it's a terrible thing to know I'll never see Les again.'

This wasn't true. Les came into town every Wednesday night, after the new hops mash had been poured into the pond, got disgustingly drunk and cleared out before dawn.

Lots of people saw him, but he didn't do any more harm so nobody bothered about him.

He went on doing this for five years. Then the brewery closed down, there was no hops mash, and nothing more was seen of Les.

But even to this day I cannot go out to the bush without worrying that I might blunder into the clutches of a huge, red, drink-crazed kangaroo who may well be bearing a grudge against me.

# TROUBLE BREWING

## Claude Morris

He came walking through the forest in the summer's glaring
    sun.
In his left hand was a bottle—in the other was a gun.
His beard was wild and bushy and his hair was shaggy too,
His old straw hat was full of holes, where tufts of hair came
    through.
I stood and waited for him as he came with steady stride,
And I studied his appearance till he soon was by my side.
He wasn't old, nor was he young, but somewhere in between,
And his heavy eyebrows almost hid his eyes of greyish green.
Then he handed me the bottle—'You must have a drink,'
    he said.
And I heard him cock the rifle, and he aimed it at my head.
'Yes, take a swig of my home brew, and you may be the first
To have a chance of trying out my recipe for thirst.'
And the rifle never wavered as it pointed straight at me,
And that close-up gaping barrel was a nasty thing to see.
I lifted up the bottle with a very shaky hand,
And a silent prayer to Heaven, as I followed his command.
I swallowed twice, and God above; that brew had come from
    Hell,
And I know my head exploded, and it drowned my dying
    yell.

I fell upon the dusty ground and grovelled there in pain,
Vowing he could shoot me, but I wouldn't drink again.
When the pain and shock receded, and I staggered to
     my feet,
'It was AWFUL—it was AWFUL,' I could hear my voice
     repeat.
Then I heard the brewer speaking, and he said, 'Yes, I agree—
Now give me back that bottle—and you hold the gun on me.'

# CHAMPAGNE AFTER THE RACES [FROM *HERE'S LUCK*]

**Lennie Lower**

> 'The only cure for a real hangover is death.'
>
> Robert Benchley, c.1930

The waiter coasted down to our table and pulled up with the silence of a Rolls-Royce hearse.

'Yessir?'

'A bottle of champagne, waiter,' ordered Stanley.

'Two bottles,' I put in.

The waiter's eyes glistened.

'Three bottles!' declared Stanley.

'Four no-trumps!' cried the waiter.

We stared at him.

'Sorry, sir,' he stammered. 'Pardon—forgot myself. Three bottles. Yessir.'

Stanley tapped his forehead as the man hurried away.

'Bridged,' he muttered pityingly; 'probably from birth.'

I nodded. I had seen too much of that sort of thing to pity the man. In the early days of my married life Agatha had threatened to divorce me for failing to lead the ten of diamonds. By some outrageous whim of a malicious fate we subsequently won the rubber and she stayed with me. I have never played the game since.

The champagne enlivened me. It thrilled and uplifted me like the fangs of a bull ant. Champagne is another symbol of achievement.

It puts a laurel wreath back among the rest of the shrubs. If head-aches were created for any practical purpose, it was to show the glory of champagne, to emphasise the beauty of the rose by the magnitude of its thorns. And we had five bottles altogether.

It was with great difficulty that the waiter and I managed to carry Stanley out to a taxi some time later. It would have been easy, only the fool waiter, muddling round with his end of Stanley, made me lose my balance and fall to the floor several times before reaching the footpath. The man was obliging enough and I gave him a handful of pound notes as some slight recompense for his trouble, urging him at the same time to bank some. He offered to go in the taxi with us and wanted to brush me down. I couldn't stand for the brushing down. Positively couldn't stand for it.

We left the restaurant, with the waiter standing in the doorway gazing sadly after us, as though he had missed an opportunity to relieve his fellow-men.

I forget how we got home, and how it came about that we both decided to sleep on the doormat instead of in bed. Probably it was a hot night. I do not indulge in the stupidity of cluttering up my mind with the memory of insignificant details and I am unable to remember anything about it.

The milkman disturbed me in the morning and I had hardly snuggled back on to the mat when the man who delivers the morning papers struck me in the ear with a deliberately aimed *Herald*.

By the time the postman arrived Stanley was awake and I sent him to the gate for the letters. There were three of them and, as a number of female broadcasters in the terrace opposite were hanging out of their windows like dogs' tongues, we retired into the house before opening the letters.

Stanley flung them on the kitchen table and we sat down. Only one was addressed to me and that was from the Easy Payment Company. Easy payment; the savage irony of the term!

It was a final notice to the effect that they would remove the gramophone if payment was not made within seven days. I filed it away among the other final notices, wondering why the postman had bothered to deliver the thing. Perhaps the drain was full. I resolved to speak to him about it.

I chewed my fingernails and looked across at Stanley. He was looking at me and holding his forehead on with both hands.

'Here,' I said, 'go and get five pounds' worth of aspirin tablets for yourself.'

His mouth flickered in a feeble smile.

'Aw, gee! Yes. Aspirin tablets.' He pulled himself to his feet and plodded to the door.

'Aspirins!' he gasped, fumbling with the handle.

The telephone bell rang with a piercing tingle that set my brains beating against my forehead.

Stanley groaned, and staggering to the phone lifted the receiver off.

'Oh, go on,' he moaned in a stricken voice.

A moment of silence.

'Oh, Daisy! Oh, I'm splendid, thanks. Dad? Yes. He's in the kitchen. I'll call him.'

'I'm not in!' I shouted.

'Hello. He's not in. Yes, he was in the kitchen a while ago. Yes. Call him a bit later. Good-bye.'

He dropped the receiver on the floor and dragged his feet toward the front door.

'Going out, Stanley?' I called.

'I think so,' he replied weakly. 'I'm flickering.'

The door slammed behind him and I pressed my forehead against the gas stove. The touch of the cold metal was like the hand of a faith-healer. It was uncomfortable kneeling on the floor with my head to the stove, so I lifted the door off it and carried it into the bedroom and lay down on it.

# MY WIFE

David Nicholson

I met my wife in the pub last night,
I couldn't believe she was there.
She's supposed to be home looking after the kids,
Not knockin' back pots for a dare!
I told her she shouldn't be drinking.
She replied, 'Well, I don't give a damn,
And actually I'm not as far gone
As most thinkle peep that I am!'
It was funny the way that her mood changed,
Going home 'neath a star-laden sky,
She went all soppy and sheepish
And looked longingly into me eye.
I placed her head on my shoulder
And I told her she looked really sweet.
And we made our way home in the moonlight,
(Someone else helped to carry her feet!)

# MY FIRST LITERARY LUNCH

## 'The Sandman'

> 'Never trust a man who doesn't drink.'
>
> Barry Humphries, 1965

The following alcoholic adventure coincided with my first ever book deal. I won't mention the publisher, or the person's name, but let's say he's a commissioning editor well-known for his liquid exploits. For convenience's sake, I'll call him Stan.

I, that is Sandman, Sandy, or me, am invited to lunch by Stan to discuss the possibility of signing a book deal with his company.

It's a tradition in literary circles that before being signed you're wined and dined. So it's arranged that I meet Stan at the Watson's Bay pub at twelve noon to discuss the deal over lunch.

I'm fifteen minutes late; I'm only a minor celebrity, I can't keep people waiting much longer than that without causing offence.

Stan, in his forties, salt and pepper hair, medium build housed in a laconic demeanour, is sitting at an outside table with a Crown lager standing guard in front of him like a taciturn grenadier. As I join him he suggests a quick beer while we order some wine and, even though the taste of toothpaste is still dominating my mouth, I accept his kind offer. Stan, very near the end of his first beer, orders another one so I'm not left drinking alone. He also orders wine to go with the meal.

It's unseasonably warm and the combination of beer and wine in the afternoon sun soon takes its toll. At the conclusion of our first bottle of wine I'm full of confidence. I tell Stan I can deliver three novellas in two years, no trouble. I'm having difficulty attaching the gs to my -ing words, but I seem to know what I'll be doing in two years' time.

Stan is one beer in front of me and shows no sign of slurring. He's like a cricketer who bowls perfect slower balls with no change in action. As Stan becomes more intoxicated, he appears to be stone-cold sober.

The main meal finishes but there are sweets and a second bottle of wine to negotiate. By now it's pushing 2.30 p.m. and we're directly in the sun. As those who have dined at Watson's Bay Hotel will be aware, the afternoon sun shines directly on the outdoor eating area.

The effect of summer sunshine on drinkers is well documented. Apparently it's the same as having three quick schooners on top of what you've already had, spinning around after you scull home brew or drinking wine from a wine bag: you get drunk much quicker.

When we finish the meal and the second bottle of wine, Stan suggests we retire to the front bar and kick on. By now six glasses of wine, a beer and three hours of sunshine have seen me well and truly over the plimsoll.

During the next two hours I consume five schooners of New and Stan drains six. (Since I'm lagging behind, Stan takes matters into his own hands and orders another beer for himself.) As I watch him I realise that nothing looks more natural than Stan in a public bar, studying the racing guide with a beer in front of him and a gasper resting on his lips like a self-conscious teenager leaning on a wall. I soon realise that if I don't come up with an excuse to escape I'll find myself bum up over the washing basket sometime tonight because it'll be the closest thing I can find when I know I can't make the toilet.

I don't want to appear weak because I know writers are cele-brated for holding their grog, so I come up with a good escape; I tell Stan I have an earache. I buy another round so it seems like I'm a good bloke, but I keep referring to my ear to make my excuse appear more legit. So we finish the round and Stan drops me home in a cab. I'm gone, but I'm not wearing the whirlybird shirt, as my aunt Coral often described people who'd drunk too much.

Within half an hour I'm in an alcoholic coma on my two-seater lounge, but while I grapple with broken sleep, Stan's legendary adventures continue.

I meet Stan quite a few times over the next few months and he eventually fills me in on what happened over the rest of that evening. This account is my own understanding of Stan's shared memories.

Stan's next port of call is the home of some Greek friends in Bondi Junction. He stays there until around 9 p.m. drinking beer and retsina. That's four more hours of drinking on top of his six glasses of wine, two Crownies and seven schooners at the Watson's Bay Hotel. Let's say, and I'm being conservative, he has six beers and three glasses of retsina at Bondi Junction. Let's say that puts him at nine glasses of wine and fifteen beers by 9 p.m.

His next stop is the Tea Gardens Hotel, Bondi Junction. The Tea Gardens is an old-fashioned pub. The public bar has all the hallmarks of a bygone era: tiles, polished wood and that sepia light that gives you the feeling a boy with rickets may come through any minute wheeling a barrow full of rabbits.

Stan is a lover of pub culture; in fact, he has written a book on the subject. He is a wonderful listener and has no trouble assimilating with strangers. He attaches himself to a group of drinkers, some of whom he knows by sight. One is a well-known actor, most of the others are the actor's cronies.

Stan is soon fully accepted into the alcoholic circle and, inevitably, someone asks what he does for a living. Stan truthfully, but perhaps foolishly, replies that he's a commissioning editor for a major publishing house.

Suddenly it appears that everybody in the group is working on a book, or has an idea for a book that will sell a million copies.

One chap says he has a great idea for a tennis book. Stan tells the chap, probably more frankly than he would normally do at the office, that tennis books never sell and he'd never be interested in publishing one.

An argument erupts, with the would-be author yelling at Stan that he doesn't know Arthur from Martha and he should piss off. Sensing a disruption in the ranks, the well-known actor intervenes. There is a heated exchange, which ends in an undignified scuffle. When a wild punch is thrown and misses Stan by millimetres, causing his fringe to pulsate like the throat of a courting frog, Stan no longer feels welcome. He picks up his opinions and heads off into the night.

The next stop on Stan's alcoholic odyssey is his dad's place at Five Dock. Time, around midnight. Let's say Stan lasted an hour and a half at the Tea Gardens. Let's say Stan had five schooners. Let's say that places him at twenty beers and nine glasses of wine in twelve hours. It seems that Stan's father also likes a drink and, despite being ill, he is happy to keep his son company until they run out of alcohol sometime around 3 a.m.

Let's say between midnight and 3 a.m. there's time for five beers and a couple of scotches. Let's also say Stan's probably feeling bloated by this stage because once you've drunk that much beer it's difficult to keep putting liquid in.

Perhaps Stan's stomach is designed like the *Titanic*, with a series of watertight compartments to stop him going down; at 3 a.m., neither man is satisfied their night is over. Father and son decide to go to a nearby hotel and take advantage of its twenty-four-hour licence.

With his dad, who is still dressed in PJs and dressing-gown, Stan makes the one-kilometre journey to the pub, where he is still able to remain upright and communicate well enough to order more drinks.

The publican says on their arrival that he doesn't mind Stan's father coming down the pub when he looks so ill because he's a regular, but he asks could he please not come down in his PJs anymore because he scares the other drinkers.

Stan and his dad drink until it's getting light and then Stan, devoted publishing man that he is, says that he fully intends to go to work. He's done it before and he can do it again. So Stan and his dad weigh anchor and cast off for the walk home.

Now, when you're really drunk, a one-kilometre walk can feel like a round-the-world voyage. From all reports, the trip home was rough going for Stan, and both he and his dad made rather heavy weather of it. Let's say from 3.30 a.m. to 5.30 a.m. they managed four beers and two scotches; that puts Stan at twenty-three beers, nine wines and four or five scotches.

As father and son tack into the stiff breeze it all becomes too much for Stan's dad; despite Stan holding onto him, Dad falls overboard. As Stan attempts to help his father back into the boat, a passing motorist sees a drunk standing over a much older drunk who is dressed in pyjamas, dressing-gown and slippers. It's 5.45 a.m. and the passing motorist finds the scene rather disturbing.

The passing motorist pulls over, gets out of his car, grabs Stan, yanks him off his father, shakes him violently and pushes him away, accusing him in no uncertain terms of trying to roll a poor defenceless wino.

Stan's communication skills are by now somewhat impaired and it takes a while for him to convince the Good Samaritan that he is only trying to help his father get home.

True to his word, Stan makes it to work. In fact he's early, so with time up his sleeve and in need of something to offset the sensations in his stomach, he ventures to the canteen for a sausage sandwich. Then, like a wild animal that removes its kill from view, Stan drags his sandwich back to his office.

Now, a sausage sandwich in oily wrapping paper inside a paper bag is like a Rubik's Cube to a drunk man. It's at this point of the story, as Stan struggles with his sandwich and strains to keep his head upright, that a colleague sticks his head through the door of Stan's office and notices Stan floating there like a specimen in formaldehyde.

The colleague says, 'Stan . . . Stan, mate . . . I think you should go home.' And that's exactly what Stan does.

It's easy to see why Stan is so successful. He works such long hours, his staff really care about him and he can take advice.

# MODERATION

## Victor Daley ('Creeve Roe')

I do not wish for wealth
Beyond a livelihood;
I do not ask for health
Uproariously good.
I do not care for men
To point with pride at me;
A model citizen
I do not wish to be.
I have no dream bizarre
Of strange erotic joy;
I want no avatar
Of Helena of Troy.
I do not crave the boon
Of Immortality;
I do not want the moon,
Not yet the rainbow's key.
I do not yearn for wings,
Or fins to swim the sea;
I merely want the things
That are not good for me.

# THIN ICE

## Russell Hannah/Jim Haynes

> 'Give strong drink unto him that is ready to perish.'
>
> Proverbs 31:6

Many years ago, in my youth, I was a painter for the Public Works Department and one of our jobs was to travel the state painting small bush schools. We worked in gangs of two and, in general, it was a good job.

The pay wasn't great but we received a pretty good 'living away from home' allowance, most of which we were able to save, as the headmaster would generally let us camp in the weather shed.

Of course, we got to see the inside of many country pubs where we happily contributed our living expenses to the Publican's Retirement Fund.

Now, one time we had to paint the school at a little place called Bardalungra. Bardalungra consisted of a few houses, a pub, a garage and general store combined and, of course, the obligatory one-teacher school. Bardalungra was a place destined for oblivion.

There was, of course, one more building, and that was the railway station. The station was small. A weatherboard waiting room attached to a signal box which contained all those mysterious levers that enable trains to pass when there's a single line.

Not that trains ever passed much at Bardalungra. It was a branch line that was serviced by a 'mixed', a goods train with a passenger carriage attached. The carriage was for those travellers who either had plenty of time for their journey or, like us, had a government rail warrant.

The old trundler was not noted for speed. It was also one of those trains which, for reasons I could never understand, would stop at irregular intervals. It would stop at sidings that barely existed, or even in what seemed to be open paddocks, and just stay there for a while.

The train only ran four times a week, except in harvest time. Then a few trains were used to cart barley and wheat. That was the only time there was any other traffic on the line.

Well, my mate and myself caught the train to Bardalungra one stinking-hot day. It was one of those days when you dream of swimming pools and cold beer. The only 'air conditioning' available was to open the windows, but the air outside was hotter than inside, that dry heat of summer in western New South Wales.

The irony of it all was that we had six bottles of beer with us that we bought the night before at a pub in Moree. We'd bought a dozen and for some reason still had six left when we finally hit the sack. Unfortunately, they were at least as hot as the air in the carriage, so we'd put off drinking them 'til we could find some suitable refrigeration.

Not surprisingly, we were the only people in the carriage. We soon struck up a conversation with the guard, as you always did on country trains back then. He was a large, friendly character with a florid face, the kind of bloke who looked like he might like a cold drink on a hot day, or any other day for that matter. He soon left the guard's van and joined us. It seemed he liked a bit of company, there being very few people travelling on the line, and it wasn't long before he knew all there was to know about us and we knew all about him.

It also wasn't long before he noticed our six large bottles of beer sitting on the seat. 'I see you boys have got a bit of the good liquid refreshment there,' he said. 'Are you going teetotal today?'

Now, our throats were pretty dry and our heads were a bit heavy from the previous night. We explained that, as much as we'd love a beer, we couldn't bring ourselves to drink beer that was quite so hot.

'I can fix you up, lads,' he said. 'I've got some ice in the van—next stop I'll pop back and bring some up.'

As luck would have it, the next stop wasn't far away. He soon disappeared back to his van and returned with a billy can half full of ice. Before too long we had the water glasses down from the carriage wall and were happily into our first bottle of cold beer. Naturally, the guard joined us. After all, it was a hot day.

It seemed that our new mate the guard had an endless supply of ice. At every stop he'd go back to his van and return with more ice in the billy. He wasn't a bad drinker either. He certainly managed to put away his fair share of our beer.

After a while we were on our last bottle and feeling quite affectionate towards our new mate, the railways, and the world in general. We were also regretting that we didn't have another six bottles left over from the night before. When we expressed this opinion to the guard, he remarked that it was probably a good thing—as he was about to run out of ice.

Perhaps it was about then that I really began to wonder where this seemingly endless supply of ice had come from.

It didn't take long to find out.

The train soon made another of its interminable stops at a small siding which had a name that thankfully I forget. The guard had left us to do 'a bit of work' in his van.

As I leaned idly out the window, my belly full of cold beer, I noticed a black panel van and two well-dressed blokes standing by the siding. 'That's funny,' I thought to myself, 'that van looks like a hearse.'

I soon realised what 'bit of work' the guard had returned to his van to do. As I watched, the doors of the guard's van opened. The two well-dressed blokes and the guard lifted a coffin out of the train and into the back of the black panel van.

It was then that I knew where the ice had come from.

# McCARTHY'S BREW

## George Essex Evans

The team of Black McCarthy crawled adown the Norman
    road,
The ground was bare, the bullocks spare, and grievous was
    the load,
The brown hawks wheeled above them and the heatwaves
    throbbed and glowed.
With lolling tongues and bloodshot eyes and sinews all
    astrain,
McCarthy's bullocks staggered on across the sun-cracked
    plain,
The waggon lumbered after with the drivers raising Cain.
Three mournful figures sat around the campfire's fitful glare,
McKinlay Jim and 'Spotty' and McCarthy's self were there,
But their spirits were so dismal that they couldn't raise a
    swear!
'Twas not the long, dry stage ahead that made those bold
    hearts shrink,
The drought-cursed ground, the dying stock, the water thick
    as ink,
But, the drinking curse was on them and they had no grog
    to drink!
Then with a bound up from the ground McCarthy jumped
    and cried:

''Tis vain! 'Tis vain! I go insane. These pangs in my inside!
Some sort of grog, for love of God, invent, concoct, provide!'
McKinlay Jim straight answered him: 'Those lotions, sauce
    and things
Should surely make a brew to slake these thirstful sufferings,
A brew that slakes, a brew that wakes and burns and bucks
    and stings.'
Down came the cases from the load—they wrenched them
    wide with force.
They poured and mixed and stirred a brew that would have
    killed a horse,
Cayenne, painkiller, pickles, embrocation, Worcester sauce!
Oh wild and high and fierce and free the orgy rose that night;
The songs they sang, the deeds they did, no poet could indite;
To see them pass that billy round, it was a fearsome sight.
The dingo heard them and with tail between his legs he fled!
The curlew saw them and he ceased his wailing for the dead!
Each frightened bullock on the plain went straightway off
    his head!
Alas! And there are those who say that at the dawn of day
Three perforated carriers round a smouldering campfire lay:
They did not think McCarthy's brew would take them in
    that way!
McCarthy's teams at Normanton no more the Gulf men see.
McCarthy's bullocks roam the wilds exuberant and free;
McCarthy lies, an instance of preserved anatomee!
Go, take the moral of this rhyme, which in deep grief I write:
Don't ever drink McCarthy's brew. Be warned in case you
    might—
Gulf whisky kills at twenty yards, but this stuff kills at sight!

# COURT DAY AT BILLY BILLY

**Anonymous (*The Bulletin*, 1896)**

> 'To alcohol! The cause of ... and solution to ...
> all of life's problems.'
>
> Matt Groening, 1990

The court house interior was almost bare of furniture, the walls were unlined and the weather-boards gaped here and there, so that the grasshoppers jumped in and out at their pleasure. Their worships (two of them) sat on a small form behind a pine table, the prisoner hung over a deal railing about eighteen inches from the wall, and Constable O'Toole stood near, reciting the villainies of the accused in a thick, monotonous, unintelligible brogue.

It was a day in Gehenna: the shrill, ringing whirr of the locusts filled the air for miles around, a bird chipped its beak sharply on the iron roof, and a tall, attenuated goat stood in the doorway, supinely observing the proceedings of the court, and emitting an occasional contemptuous 'bah'.

But the court (that is the two magistrates presiding) seemed oblivious to everything but the dreadful heat and its own sorrows.

Half of the court, open-mouthed, followed the meanderings of a lame bull ant on the table, between intervals of sleep, and occasionally stirred the insect up with a straw to add to the excitement. The other half, with his head thrown back and his occiput resting on the chair rail, gazed meditatively at the roof, daydreaming of strong drinks and occasionally relapsing into a gurgling snore suggestive of a frog croaking in a ship's hold, and then pulling himself together with an effort and trying to look wise.

And all the time Constable O'Toole droned along about 'this yere mahn' who had been discovered the night previous, howling on the road 'afore widdy Johnson's' with nothing on 'barrin' th' dust, yer worships, which he'd buried hisself in'.

Prisoner was charged with drunkenness and disorderly conduct, and was a woebegone object, the Sahara incarnate. His tongue could be heard grating against his palate and he looked piteously thirsty. When the policeman had done, he put in a word or two in extenuation of his weakness, reminding their worships of the weather they had been having, and concluding with a touching and wholly ineffectual effort to expectorate.

The court felt itself called upon, and one half arose, and, steadying itself by leaning over the table, assumed a look of inhuman gravity, and said: 'Prisoner, such conducksh wholly indefensh-ible—disgrash tyer manhood. You are fined sheven daysh or twenty-four hoursh.'

Then that half sat down, with the air of a man who has done his duty by his country, and the other half arose, and, after blinking blearily for a few moments at the prisoner, with an assumption of owl-like wisdom, added: 'Sheven daysh 'r twenty-foursh hoursh, *both of you!*'

'Yesh,' corroborated the first half, rising again, '*both of you!*'

Then the court adjourned.

# A RUM COMPLAINT

## Claude Morris

The old man held out his hands that shook
Like the leaves of a wind-blown tree,
And begged the doctor for relief
From his ghastly malady.
The doctor gave him a thorough check,
With sure and competent touch.
'There's not much wrong with you,' he said,
'Except that you drink too much.'
'That's all very well,' the old bloke said—
'You can blame the grog if you will,
But it's not what I drink that's gettin' me down—
It's the bloody amount that I spill.'

# A JOURNALIST'S FUNERAL

**Anonymous (*The Bulletin*, 1889)**

> 'Here's to alcohol, the rose colored glasses
> of life.'
>
> F. Scott Fitzgerald, 1922

It was a new sensation to be in a coffin, with a hearse all to myself as the sole passenger. I had exhausted all other sensations, and this seemed to be the last. Strangely enough I was not afraid; the utterly novel experience acted upon me like hasheesh.

I actually enjoyed it in a dreamy contemplative kind of way. You will at once perceive that I was not dead at the time, or I would not be writing this now.

Two dismally shabby cabs crawled after my conveyance, and I noticed with mingled envy and indignation (so far as I could be touched by either of these feelings) that they stopped at every hotel on the road, in order that the mourners might have an opportunity of drinking my health, I suppose.

In the state of trance, for that was what it really was, in which I was at the time the mysterious faculty, sometimes vaguely called the sixth sense, must have been developed. I heard what my mourners were saying about me as plainly as if I had been sitting beside them, while the hearse went slowly grinding along the dusty road to the cemetery.

'He was nobody's enemy but his own—poor Jack!' said Mr O'Connell, blowing through the stem of his pipe to clear it. And out of the glass windows of the hearse, paid for, as I discovered afterwards, by a generous theatrical manager whom I have written slightingly of on many occasions, but who, thank heaven, still survives to be repaid by my borrowing a tenner from him the first time we meet, I saw, through all intervening obstacles, this stout, dark little man making rings (mourning rings, I suppose) with his tumbler on the bar counter of the hotel.

And at once there flashed upon me a memory. It was a moonlit night in summer six years ago, I was on board one of the small steamers that run from Circular Quay to Mosman Bay. Sitting beside me was the brightest and lightest writer I have met in these lands. He was not given to serious reflection as a general thing, and I was somewhat surprised when he turned to me suddenly and said in a tone of gloom so intense that it was almost grotesque: 'They may say anything they please about me when I am dead, so long as they don't say "He was nobody's enemy but his own."'

And that is precisely what they did say, word for word. He has been dead for some years now, but his imitators have been many and one or two have almost succeeded in catching something of the ring of his style.

We, that is to say, the hearse, the undertaker's men and myself, were about a mile ahead of my mourners just then. I noticed them coming out of the fourth public house on the road, wiping their lips.

'Well, there's no use crying over spilt milk, boys,' (nobody was crying that I could see, so this must have been a mere *façon de parler*) said the sub-editor of the paper to which I used to contribute most of my work. 'He's dead, and that's all there is about it. Brush away those tears!' (Spoken melodramatically, there were no tears.) 'I've got to get out of here to start on my work.'

Which he at once proceeded to do, and went on his way with long strides and a slight lurch.

And this man I had considered a genuine, if not particularly demonstrative, friend of mine.

The miserable tail of two cabs, looking like desperate bailiffs on wheels, followed me until it came to the next pub. Then it detached itself again and the occupants shambled out. Presently a voice said, 'Poor old boy! Here's luck to him wherever he goes. He was never afraid of hot weather.'

'Not while there was any drink around,' remarked Jim McCann, draining his pint of shandy-gaff at one splendid swig.

'Plenty where he's going,' said McNab, the commercial man, 'he always liked his liquor hot.'

He then began to tell a string of the most outrageous fictions concerning what he and I had done when we had been on 'sprees' together, things which, if they had ever happened, would have got us into gaol or the lunatic asylum half a dozen times over. Yet he actually intended these astounding fabrications as a tribute to my memory! It was his idea of a funeral eulogium.

'Well, gentlemen,' said the first voice, 'I must leave you here. I enjoy a spree as much as anybody, but I have some special work to do, and I can't neglect it. See the old boy planted truly and well.'

And *he* went off. 'Nice lot of heartbroken mourners *I* have,' I thought.

My old friend Tom Dorgan, who had never said a word all this time, except that it was a fine day for a funeral, then observed, 'The mourners are thinning out, Flynn.'

'Yes,' replied Flynn (a kindly cynic in his way), 'they mostly do at the end of any funeral of this sort.'

It was an amiable characteristic of Flynn's that when he had an audience cooped up in a corner (and what better corner could be found than a mourning cab?) he held that audience at his mercy, which wasn't much.

'You see,' he went on, 'the poor old boy *had* to die. He didn't *time* his drinks, you know. All the time was his time when liquor was about. Besides, the strain upon his intellect in writing comic paragraphs was enough to kill an emu. I'm beginning to feel it tell upon me, myself.'

'I want to get out at South Melbourne,' said a husky voice from the corner of the cab.

It appeared that this gentleman had got into one of the cabs while the mourners and drivers were in a pub (saying what a fine fellow I was) and, being in a somewhat intoxicated condition, had mistaken it for one of the cabs that plied on the road to where he lived.

'I'd like to inform you, sir, that you are at a funeral, and respect shall and will be shown to the illustrious dead, or there will be trouble,' said McGinnis Walker, of the Press Bureau, speaking for the first time. And with that McNab hustled the gentleman violently into the road. As soon as he had picked himself up he tore off his coat, threw his hat down, and challenged the entire funeral, offering to smash up the whole party.

But the funeral passed on and left him prancing around in a ring and defying everything within the circle of the horizon to come on and be ground into powder.

Soon after another mourner left. He said he would be late for dinner if he didn't get out at once and his wife would be very angry if such a tragedy occurred. And *he* departed.

'He was not a bad fellow, he was my best friend, boys, this has cut me up terribly. Have you got a match, Flynn?' said McNab.

'He stole two of my best original stories,' growled McGinnis Walker, 'but I forgive him, now he's dead. I stole them myself.'

When we arrived at the grave there was only one mourner—McGinnis Walker, and he was asleep in a corner of the cab. All the rest had either got out or fallen out on the way.

Tom had been overcome by his grief at the last pub, and McNab had been taken in charge by a policeman for offering in a public place to fight anybody who would dare to say that I wasn't the best all-round genius that had lived since the time of Shakespeare.

I felt three dull thuds on my coffin lid.

'Mother of Glory!' I yelled, 'what's this?'

I awoke to find that about a yard of the bedroom ceiling had fallen upon me.

I wonder if this will be anything like what will occur when I die? I don't care in the least so long as, in the words of my friend gone before, they don't say, 'He was Nobody's Enemy but his Own.'

# THE PINTS THAT I'VE REFUSED

### E.G. Murphy ('Dryblower')

From out the mulga shade I look,
Across the grave of years,
To days when I unwilling took
Small shandy-gaffs, not beers.
And when the stars upon me stare
From out the dusky vault,
There steals along the heated air
The scent of hops and malt.
I conjure up the liquid feast
In brewery cellars cool,
Where oft I've played, amidst the yeast,
The dashed teetotal fool!
My punishment is that of Cain,
My soul is self-accused,
As hour by hour I count again
The pints that I've refused.
At dusk I do not weep or curse
As on my swag I sit,
And vote this world a trifle worse
Than deep Gehenna's pit.
I do not sigh for rippling rills,
That babble through the ferns,
Ah, no, for flowing frothy swills

My thirsty thorax yearns!
I recollect the sprees that irked
When shanties ran with shick;
And, as I think of drinks I've shirked,
My mental-self I kick.
Yes, here amidst a beerless drought
My heart with grief is bruised
When I, in fancy, figure out
The pints that I've refused.
Hot Hell might just consist, I think,
Of long and pintless years,
Where no poor sinful soul may drink
His fill of cooling beers.
The burning brimstone and the torch
May be for mulga men,
But grant, oh Satan, as I scorch,
A tiddley now and then.
Still, if the devil will not give
What I'm on earth denied,
I may at last decide to live
Wherein no souls are fried;
And when Saint Peter at the door
My passport has perused,
He'll put me, p'rhaps, where I may score
The pints that I've refused.

# DRINKS WITH A KICK IN THEM

## Lennie Lower

> 'I am prepared to admit some merit in every alcoholic beverage ever devised by the incomparable brain of man.'
>
> H.L. Mencken, 1956

The President of the Housewives' Association says that she does not believe in cocktail drinking and could, if necessary, produce a drink with a 'kick' in it, from fruit.

Anticipating, we have evolved a few recipes to suit all tastes.

*Banana Flutter*

Take one banana, slice, and put into glass. Take half a coconut and beat the milk into a stiff froth. Mix briskly and serve. The 'kick' is obtained by standing on one foot on the skin of the banana and leaning forward while pouring the drink down the back of the neck.

Then we have the *Flying Mule*

Take half-dozen raspberries, being careful to remove the seeds, also the sound. Mash lightly with hammer. Mix with a little ice-water, and add seeds slowly, one at a time, until you are so thirsty that you'd drink anything. Now take a red-hot nail, and dip it smartly into the mixture, removing it almost immediately. Drink nail.

*The Watermelon Whoopee*

Take one large watermelon, cut in half. Hollow out one half and place contents in wash-basin. Save seeds from other half. Place in wash-basin one small cup of gramophone needles, half-pint of sulphuric acid. Drink before bottom falls out of wash-basin.

A similar mixture is the *Hangover Blues*

The watermelon is put into the wash-basin as before, but covered with crushed ice. The hollowed-out portion is then quarter-filled with crushed ice and placed over the head, taking care to pull it well down over the forehead. The face is then laid gently in the wash-basin.

It will be seen from the above recipes that the uses of fruit as a drink are practically unlimited. Furthermore, most fruit is full of vitamins.

These need not worry the hostess, however, as they can easily be detected by the small holes in the outside of the skin, and this part can be cut out.

And don't forget, all these drinks have a kick.

The careful hostess should warn her guests of this danger.

# BLUEY BRINK

**Anonymous**

There once was a shearer, by name Bluey Brink,
A devil for work and a demon for drink;
He'd shear his two hundred a day without fear,
And drink without blinking four gallons of beer.
Now Jimmy the barman who served out the drink,
He hated the sight of this here Bluey Brink,
He stayed much too late, and he came much too soon,
At evening, at morning, at night and at noon.
One morning as Jimmy was cleaning the bar,
With sulphuric acid he kept in a jar,
In comes Old Bluey a'yelling with thirst:
'Whatever you've got, Jim, just hand me the first!'
Now it ain't down in history, it ain't down in print,
But that shearer drank acid with never a wink,
Saying, 'That's the stuff, Jimmy! Well, strike me stone dead,
This'll make me the ringer of Stevenson's shed!'
Now all that long day as he served out the beer,
Poor Jimmy was sick with his trouble and fear;
Too worried to argue, too anxious to fight,
Seeing the shearer a corpse in his fright.
When early next morning, he opened the door,
Then along came the shearer, asking for more,
With his eyebrows all singed and his whiskers deranged,

And holes in his hide like a dog with the mange.
Says Jimmy, 'And how did you like the new stuff?'
Says Bluey, 'It's fine, but I ain't had enough!
It gives me great courage to shear and to fight,
But why does that stuff set my whiskers alight?
I thought I knew drink, but I must have been wrong,
For that stuff you gave me was proper and strong;
It set me to coughing, you know I'm no liar,
*And every cough set my whiskers on fire!'*

# HOW SEXY REX CLEARED THE BAR

**Jim Haynes**

> 'There aren't many countries in the world where people get the DTs on beer. Australia is one of them.'
>
> Dr E. Cunningham Dax, 1969

Sexy Rex was a shearers' cook, or had been . . . or said he had been.

When I knew him he spent most of his time *telling* people about being a shearers' cook—from a corner of the bar at the Tatts, or the Royal—or at odd times when his liver was having a bad day, from a table near the window in the Paragon Cafe. Maybe he'd never been a shearers' cook at all. I never met anyone who remembered him being one. There were plenty of people, however, who remembered him *telling* them about being one.

Being a shearers' cook doesn't seem much to boast about, or spend most of your time reminiscing about. Most blokes I know who had been shearers' cooks kept pretty quiet about it and found other things to talk about. They certainly found other things to boast about. But Sexy Rex *liked* to boast about being a shearers' cook.

He was probably called 'Sexy Rex' because he was the least sexy person imaginable, or simply because it was the first rhyme that sprang to mind—or perhaps a bit of both.

Anyway, Sexy Rex walked with a pronounced limp, when he walked at all. He didn't walk much, for two reasons. Firstly because of his pronounced limp and secondly because his main claim to fame, his real skill in life, was cadging lifts from one pub to the other, because he walked with a pronounced limp.

No one ever questioned that Rex's limp was a result of 'the war'. But the funny thing was that he never talked about 'the war' or claimed to have fought in World War II. He'd arrived in the district after the war, complete with his pronounced limp so I guess everyone just assumed that he acquired the limp in the war.

He didn't wear an RSL badge and he didn't march in the Anzac Day parade because of his limp. He did do his share of 'anzacing' at the pub after the march but his reminiscences, even on Anzac Day, were invariably about being a shearers' cook.

It was actually Spanner Toole who cleared the bar at the Royal, and that was because he was fed up with 'Boof' Simpson and Billy O'Shea reminding him about the belting they'd given him the night before outside the town's other pub, the Tatts.

Now the hiding Spanner had copped the night before outside the Tatts was pretty much Spanner's fault. He could be fairly annoying when he tied one on and he had this bad habit of digging up a little 'local history' and broadcasting it around the bar, airing other people's dirty laundry in public.

Let's be honest, Spanner was a nasty piece of work when he'd had a few. There weren't many drinkers at the Tatts who had any time for him when he was in that condition. On Friday night at the Tatts he was getting no encouragement from the other drinkers, but he expounded his theories nonetheless and anyone who was in the bar couldn't help but hear them.

On this particular occasion his theory concerned the alleged results of an alleged relationship between his own father, now deceased, and Nola Simpson.

Nola Simpson was not deceased but very much alive and kicking. What's more she was Boof's mother and Billy's aunt. Boof and Billy were quite willing to do the kicking necessary to defend her honour, especially when the person getting kicked was Spanner Toole.

By all accounts Nola's son and nephew had done a pretty good job of defending her honour in her absence outside the Tatts that night.

The resulting fight outside the Tatts had, by all accounts, not been a pretty sight and Spanner was an even less pretty sight than usual when he arrived at the Royal for a recuperative drink the next day.

Boof and Billy were already drinking at the Royal when Spanner arrived; they had naturally been barred from the Tatts for giving Spanner a hiding.

Boof and Billy held no particular grudge against Dougie, the Tatts' publican, about being barred from the Tatts, even though they had not started the fight. They pretty much accepted that, if you got involved in a Friday night 'incident' and then gave someone a hiding outside a pub, you would be barred from that pub for a time. So Boof and Billy were drinking at 'the other pub' and having a few bets with Fancy Youngman, the SP bookie, when Spanner arrived.

In charge of the bar that day was Harold Davis, known as 'Happy Harold' to the desperate drinkers who frequented the Royal, because he never smiled. He lived alone in a bit of a shanty on the edge of town, in a bend of the river known to locals as Happy Valley.

Happy Harold was a 'Jimmy Woodser', a solitary drinker who was always sober when he was at work behind the bar at the Royal, and never sober any other time. He had a dry wit, told a good story and got drunk as soon as he finished a shift.

It wasn't Spanner Toole alone who cleared the bar at the Royal that Saturday afternoon, it was a combination of Spanner and the old side-by-side double-barrelled shotgun he got out from under the seat of his ute and carried back into the bar. He did this because he was fed up with Boof Simpson and Billy O'Shea insulting him and reminding him about the belting they had given him the night before outside the Tatts.

'When Spanner and the shotgun entered the bar,' Harold said later, 'the bar cleared pretty quickly.'

A lot of blokes disappeared into the toilets at the end of the bar. Gender was suddenly not an issue according to Harold; the Ladies being just as popular as the Gents at that particular moment. A lot of the bar cleared into the lounge and tap room at the further end. The bar did not, oddly enough, clear into the street, perhaps because the area in the general vicinity of that door was more or less occupied by Spanner and the shotgun.

Harold was left alone in the relative safety of the area behind the bar, with the glasses piled high along it. He had simply to duck down to remove the immediate threat of being in the firing line of Spanner and his shotgun.

Which brings us to the crux of the story really. It was at that point, as he ducked down, that Harold realised he was no longer alone behind the bar. He had been joined there by Sexy Rex.

Harold says that Sexy Rex, in spite of his limp and alleged 'bad' leg, must have *cleared the bar* and the glasses stacked on it to join him in relative safety behind it.

Were we to believe Happy Harold would tell lies? Or did we choose to believe that our local crippled ex-serviceman could clear a four-foot bar, stacked with glasses, in a split second with no apparent side effects?

It was a dilemma which would concern the town longer than the current 'shotgun' crisis. Because Spanner stopped yelling abuse at the whole town in general, and Boof and Billy in particular, when the sergeant arrived a few minutes later to relieve him of the shotgun.

While Spanner climbed quietly into the paddy wagon to be taken to the lock-up, the sergeant did something quite uncharacteristic. He had Spanner's collar in one hand and the shotgun in the other and, knowing Spanner as well as he did, he assumed that Spanner would never actually *load* a shotgun and take it into the bar of the Royal. So he pointed the gun, which was cocked, at the outside brick wall of the pub, and pulled the trigger.

The marks of the pellets are still there in the brickwork today. They serve as a constant and historic reminder of Harold's amazing claim that Sexy Rex cleared the bar the day that Spanner Toole cleared the bar with the loaded shotgun.

But even Harold was forced to admit he didn't actually *see* Sexy Rex clear the bar. Perhaps Sexy Rex got behind the bar another way. None of us can imagine how, but we prefer to leave the episode in the unsolved file rather than believe that Sexy Rex was not the genuine article.

# A SONG OF LIGHT

## John Barr

There have plenty songs been written of the moonlight on
    the hill,
Of the starlight on the ocean and the sun-flecks on the rill,
But one glorious song has never fallen yet upon my ear,
'Tis a royal song of gladness of the gaslight on the beer.
I have watched an amber sunset creep across a black-faced
    bay;
I have seen the blood-flushed sunrise paint the snow one
    winter day,
But the gleam I will remember best, in lingering days to
    come,
Was a shaft of autumn radiance lying on a pint of rum.
I have seen the love stars shining through bronze hair across
    my face,
I have seen white bosoms heaving 'neath a wisp of open lace,
But resplendent yet in memory, and it seemeth brighter far,
Was a guttered candle's flicker on a tankard in a bar . . .

# ACKNOWLEDGEMENTS

My thanks to:

- Rebecca Kaiser, Tom Bailey-Smith, Leanne McGregor, Luke Causby and all at Allen & Unwin.
- Susin Chow for meticulous editing and great suggestions as always.
- Russell Hannah.
- David Nicholson for permission to use 'My Wife'.
- The estate of the late Col Wilson for permission to use 'The Morning After'.
- The estate of the late Frank Daniel for permission to use 'The Six O'clock Swells'.
- Jacqueline Kent, Stephen Abbott and the estate of the late Kenneth Cook.